Fred —
Old neighborhood buddy

Dim Sum

The Seattle ABC (American Born Chinese) Dream

Thanks! *Vera Ing*   by Vera Ing

International Examiner Press, Seattle

ISBN 978-0-615-38380-4

International Examiner

The International Examiner is a 501(c)3 nonprofit organization. It is the oldest and the only nonprofit pan-Asian American newspaper in the United States. The Examiner also publishes the Pacific Reader, the only Asian American review of books in the country. The International Examiner Press is devoted to publishing works by and about Asian Americans in the Pacific Northwest.

Cover and book design: Carmela Lim
Layout assistance and production: Debbie Louie

This is dedicated with love to my grandchildren:

Connor Ing Dougherty
Carlyn Ing Dougherty
Trevor Hwang Ing
Justine Hwang Ing

and to your future generations...

Introduction

I'm not sure when I first met Vera Ing, but I think it was probably in Chinatown during the mid-1970s, when many of us who had grown up in the community were returning to see how we might help restore its vibrancy.

It was a tumultuous time. Chinatown, in the eyes of many of the activists, was now called the International District, a nod to the new pan-Asian American identity and multicultural sensitivity that had swept from the college campuses into the innercity core. It was a time of noisy rallies at City Hall, King County and the Federal Building. There were many interminable community meetings involving a curious mix of city bureaucrats, radical student activists, elderly Chinatown residents, urban planners, young Asian attorneys, long-time shopkeepers and restaurant owners. The meetings were about how best to reclaim the neighborhood – its buildings and streets – from years of physical deterioration and neglect and to protect the residents and small businesses from the potential ravages of large-scale outside development.

Near the end of a meeting organized by the International District Improvement Association – Inter*Im, for short – and the International District Housing Alliance, I met Vera. She was easy to spot because most everyone else came to the meeting in the grunge clothing of the time: army jackets and black leather coats, blue jeans, platform shoes, long hair and mutton chop sideburns. Vera came nattily dressed in a professional businesswoman's attire. She looked out of place.

I was a student at the University of Washington and a reporter for the *International Examiner*, a new community newspaper. Vera, noticing that I was scribbling on a reporter's pad, walked up to me. She jabbed at me, a playful tone in her voice: "I hope you don't make the story too negative." I looked up, a little startled; I didn't know her and didn't quite know how to take her comment. I hadn't had a proper introduction before she had begun to lecture me about an article that I hadn't yet written.

Before I knew it, she had wrapped her arm around mine, and began walking me out of the room. "Come with me. Here's what you should write," she began. As we walked out into the street, Vera click-clacking down the sidewalk in her heels, me padding along in my army jacket and sneakers, several white-haired Chinese women shouted out to Vera in Chinese from across the street: "Ah, Vee-la!" Vera stopped. They came over and chatted with her briefly before Vera and I moved on. It was clear that people knew her, that she was deeply connected to the history of this neighborhood.

This was the first of many encounters with Vera over the years. These encounters were mostly all in Chinatown because that's where I hung out in those days, working as editor of the *International Examiner* newspaper and living in the Evergreen Apartments on Maynard Avenue during a chunk of the 1980s. Later, during my tenure as executive director of the Wing Luke Asian Museum, from 1991 to 2007, we continued to cross paths, working on many of the same issues together. Each encounter with Vera – each shared experience – deepened my understanding of her connections and her passion for this neighborhood.

Eternal optimist is an apt cliché to describe Vera. Always seeing the glass half full instead of half empty. One year – this must have been somewhere in the late 1970s – Vera helped organize a holiday arts-and-crafts bazaar in the basement of the Bush Hotel to support the small businesses that were languishing there. This "park level" of the Hotel – renamed the Bush-Asia Center to give the place the marketing sizzle of something other than a dreary old hotel in Chinatown – didn't have much foot traffic from tourists. The 1915 hotel, adjacent to Hing Hay Park, had been renovated as part of the International District community's first stab at creating a mixed-use development. There were apartments on the upper floors, nonprofit offices on the second floor and businesses down below. This was a great concept, but it would take a few more years – in a neighborhood still too ghetto to attract outsiders – to make the businesses a viable part of the formula.

During the month leading up to Christmas, Vera helped organize and staff an arts-and-crafts bazaar in this – let's call it what it was – basement. She put up garland decorations and lights, and tended to a sandwich board sign on the street that boldly proclaimed "Holiday Sale." I stopped by nearly every day to see whether much was happening with the businesses since I worked just down the street. It was always pretty dead. Not pretty dead, very dead. Despite Vera's best efforts, not many shoppers made their way inside the Bush-Asia Center. The businesses downstairs didn't survive long. But through the entire holiday season, Vera kept everybody's spirits up, walking back and forth along the corridor between the businesses, chatting with the shopkeepers and cajoling the occasional shoppers, mostly employees from social service agencies in the area, to open their wallets. On a couple days, Vera donned a Santa hat and holiday scarf, always remaining upbeat, always smiling, occasionally stepping outside to buttonhole passersby to come inside, never failing in her eternal optimism that a flood of shoppers might be just minutes away.

In 1980, Vera helped organize the first major Asian American art exhibition at the Wing Luke Museum, a show titled "Made in America," featuring established Asian American luminaries like George Tsutakawa, Andrew Chinn, Josel Namkung and Val Laigo as well as lesser known artists trying to gain visibility. Vera called up the artists one by one – no one turned her down – and through her patient efforts, she assembled this first-of-a-kind exhibition for the greater Seattle community.

This was gutsy. At the time, the Museum wasn't committed to diverging very far from its modest formula-like traditional Asian folk art shows. Asian American art was considered a less noteworthy – and certainly less profitable – realm for the Museum to venture into. But Vera's cause was to make sure that there was room for the artwork of Asians who lived here in this community. Her cause – and mine as well – was affirming the legitimacy and quality of artistic expression that blended cultural influences from Asia with those that emerged organically right here in the United States.

When Vera decided to run for a seat in the State Legislature in 1984, she asked me to help her with some practice interviews and sought my counsel so that she could clarify her positions on specific issues such as school funding, bilingual education, taxes and economic development. I remember having practice sessions with her at her Mt. Baker home. She looked like quite the candidate – usually decked out in her favorite bright red outfit purchased at Value Village for the campaign – but her snappy appearance belied her inexperience in public speaking. She would fumble with articulating her stances – she was not, by nature, a good public speaker – she was a much better one-on-one schmoozer, but she never seemed to lose heart, even under the most uncharitable tongue-lashing of friends. "Vera, what the hell are you talking about?" I would say, trying my best to steer her into a coherent sound bite. "Don't beat around the bush. Tell us what your position is. Clarity!"

During the practice sessions, I distinctly remember that she often seemed much more concerned with making sure she was a good host than whether she was doing well. Halfway into the sessions – as some of us were getting ready to throw our hands up in despair over her meandering statements – she would suddenly interject, "Anybody hungry yet? Let me fix us something to eat." She would then disappear into the kitchen, and the practice session, barely underway, would come to a premature close. I sometimes wondered silently to myself whether she really had the fire that it took to win election to office. In the end, she fell short in her bid to attain elected office, but whether she had the fire or not, all of us who were friends had some great times at her house and had been well fed and taken care of. In truth, maybe that's all that she ever really wanted.

Following her campaign, I asked her to write a column for the *International Examiner*: "Dim Sum: Bits of the Asian American Dream." The column was a hit with readers, helping her develop newfound confidence and skill in public speaking. Today, she is frequently asked to speak at community events.

One last Vera story. In the early 1980s, when I was working as editor of the *International Examiner*, living on a pauper's salary, she walked into my office one day with a blue Calvin Klein ski jacket. She had bought it on sale at the Fredrick & Nelson department store. "This is for you," she announced. "Try it on." I did – and it was a great fit. It was fully lined and had padded shoulders and was very comfortable, a cut above any other garment I had ever owned. She wanted me to wear it, she said, because she was tired of "seeing you wear that brown Metro bus driver's jacket."

I faced a heart-wrenching dilemma. The so-called Metro bus driver's jacket – a chocolate brown color with thin bands of red, green and blue near the shoulders – was a ski jacket my mother had sewn for me on the sly while she was working at Roffe's, one of the many downtown sewing factories where she toiled long hours for sweatshop wages to support our family while I was growing up. I loved the brown jacket because it, too, was comfortable. It wasn't as stylish as the one Vera had given me, but my mom had made it, and that counted for a lot.

For the next five years, I alternated between wearing the Calvin Klein jacket and my mom's brown jacket. The Calvin Klein jacket finally gave way to excessive wear – the lining began to shred – and it went to Goodwill. My mom's jacket, a little more durable, went into my basement closet, where it now languishes, waiting to be handed down to one of my two sons, whichever one wants it when they grow up.

When Vera approached me about helping her write her autobiography in 2007, I balked for a moment. I knew I would have to do a lot of editing – I used to edit her "Dim Sum" column at the *Examiner* many years ago – and I didn't know if I could commit the time to help, especially since I had just started a new teaching job at the University of Washington. But I remembered the many selfless things Vera had done for the community through the years and our shared Chinatown and International District history. And I remembered the Calvin Klein jacket which had kept me dry and warm for so many years. How could I say no?

In these following pages, Vera recounts the story of her life, from her early days in Chinatown, to the growing up years in the Central Area and her adult years in the Mt. Baker community. She talks about a lifetime of friendships in an era when enduring friendships counted for a lot more than they seem to today, and about a lifetime of service in an era when community service fueled the reclamation of distressed neighborhoods. She talks – with nostalgic fervor – about treasured cultural traditions that have nearly vanished from families that have assimilated too quickly and with careless abandon.

In telling her story, Vera does what so many of us ultimately yearn to do: pass on a personal legacy to children and grandchildren and to the generations yet unborn. But this book has value beyond simply the family story. Because of how Vera has chosen to live her life and because of what she remembers, this book is also a valuable resource for those who want to learn about Seattle neighborhood history, Chinese traditions, Chinatown-International District history, Asian American history and the Civil Rights Movement.

Finally a few acknowledgements are in order: Thanks to my research partner and co-editor Ed Echtle, Vera's husband Joey for illustrations, Carmela Lim for publication design, Debbie Louie for layout assistance and production, Gary Iwamoto for text review and fact-checking and Roger Shimomura for permission to use his artwork for the cover.

Ron Chew
Chew Communications
July 1, 2010

Golden Mountain

The Asian American Dream

Golden Mountain

The Asian American Dream

I call this book an "Asian American story." It's the story of my life, but my story is similar to that of many others of my generation. Our personal history and dreams are part of a larger saga that began in Asia and continues here in America. In looking back on our lives, many of us – approaching retirement or already retired – want to share our personal stories not just with our children and our grandchildren, but also with the community and the larger society.

I am an "ABC." This is shorthand for "American-born Chinese." I am a second-generation Chinese American. The first generation who were born in China – the community elders – have another term for us; they call us "*jook sing*." This phrase translates as "hollow bamboo," referring to Chinese Americans who don't fit totally in either the Western society or traditional Chinese society.

During my earliest years – while World War II was still raging – I lived in Seattle's segregated Chinatown. The Chinese restaurant is woven into my growing up memories. My parents owned and operated the Don Ting Café in Chinatown from the 1930s until 1960 when my mother finally sold the restaurant.

I lost my beloved father – we called him Ah Ba – when I was age seven, just after World War II. Our family had moved to Seattle's Central Area, a neighborhood immediately outside of Chinatown in the Fall of 1946. Ah Ba died in March of 1948. That area which I called home was a community of working class Blacks, Whites and Asians. I was raised there under the strong guiding hand of my mother, Ah Ma, who, like many other immigrant mothers of her

From left: Mari Elizabeth, Vera Faye, John Fisher. The Chan children, 1943 – Author's photo.

generation, demonstrated an amazing will power, resourcefulness and instinct for survival.

We lived at 1503 East Jefferson, near Providence Hospital. Growing up among other Chinese Americans, Japanese Americans and Filipino Americans, my life expanded beyond Chinatown and the International District. My friends and I pursued the American dream in our own separate ways. We were able, with hard work and perseverance, to achieve dreams that were not possible for our immigrant parents.

In recounting the story of my life, I have memories of both good times as well as hard, challenging times. But in reflecting back on my experiences, I always try to look on the bright side of things. I've always felt that this is the best way to move forward, to not linger on life's sour or tragic moments.

I grew up with three other siblings: an older sister Mari, older brother John and younger sister Helen. Our parents never told us many details about our family history. I think we all regretted not knowing more, especially about our parents' early life in China and relatives back in the old country. Mari and I even have different recollections of our childhood. But both of us agree that we have been able to achieve much more than we thought possible in our youth.

We ABCs were vaguely aware that as Chinese Americans we not only had 150 years of history in America, but we also had over 3,000 years of Chinese history that we could claim as our own. We didn't know exactly what that meant and how it related to us. Still, we felt a sense of pride in being part of that – and a sense of responsibility to uphold that tradition.

It was typical for first generation parents not to tell their ABC children much about their past. The Confucian ethics of respect and deference within the family meant you never questioned the reasoning or authority of your elders.

Ah Ba in the 1920s – Author's photo.

The first generation also wanted to protect the security of their families in America. They didn't want to tell their children the true story of the past, knowing that many Chinese came to this country illegally and probably feeling that they did not want to burden their children with the hardships of their past.

During the 1950s, the immigrant generation had to deal with McCarthyism, the Cold War and the Bamboo Curtain between the Communist People's Republic of China and a fiercely anti-Communist United States. The immigrants didn't want the government to view them as Communist sympathizers or find something wrong with their immigration papers. As a result, whenever I asked Ah Ma about specifics of our family history, she told us only that we came from a proud background and that if we stepped out of line, it would bring shame to our ancestors, family, and standing in the community.

Now that Ah Ba and Ah Ma are gone, those of us who are ABCs depend on our memories and what we've been able to retrieve through conversations with friends and personal research to construct a legacy to pass down to our children. This book is about remembering our past, and sharing some insights into the cultural practices and traditions that shaped our lives while we were growing up, whether or not we understood them at the time. Unless you are pure Native American, whether you are ABC, newcomer, mixed race ancestry or descendants of the Mayflower, your personal immigrant history is an important cornerstone of your identity and American dream.

I was born in 1940, right before the United States entered World War II. My father was born in 1889, my mother in 1899. It was the second marriage for both of them. Ah Ba had a wife and daughter in China, and Ah Ma had a husband and children there. I'm guessing that they lost their families in China by famine or war. They married in Seattle in 1933. Their ABC children – Mari, John and myself – were born in 1935, 1936 and 1940, respectively. My younger sister Helen was adopted into our family in 1949.

Ah Ba – his English name was Chan D. Kan – probably immigrated to America in the 1920s as a "merchant." Although laws barred Chinese laborers from coming to the U.S. after 1882, there were exceptions that allowed merchants to come over. Many immigrants bought

Don Ting Café, 1937
– Washington State Archives,
Puget Sound Branch.

shares in stores in the U.S. to take advantage of this loophole. My Uncle Tommy told me Ah Ba first worked in the mining camps in Idaho. Whether this is true or not, he later came to Seattle and worked for Seattle's Quong Tuck and Tuck Sing companies as a labor broker, accountant and manager.

Like most of the first Chinese immigrants to Seattle, Ah Ba came from Guangdong Province in Southeast China. He was born in Canton – now usually referred to as Guangzhou – and spoke *sam yip* or the "Three Districts" dialect, which is considered standard Cantonese. Ah Ma spoke *sze yip*, the "Four Districts" dialect, a rural village version of Cantonese. Many people considered *sam yip* better or more refined than *sze yip*. I speak my mother's dialect.

Ah Ba did beautiful calligraphy, wrote poetry and played the butterfly harp with the Luck Ngi Musical Club in Seattle for the local Chinese operas. He could also read and write rudimentary English. These skills made him a Chinatown commodity since most of the sojourner Chinese immigrants at that time only spoke Chinese and knew very little if any English.

Eventually he bought shares into the Don Ting Café (which translates as "Heaven's Grotto") on Seventh Avenue in Chinatown and later became the owner of the restaurant. In those days, nearly all Chinese worked in restaurants, groceries or laundries. Most worked in the laundries. Being a restaurant owner was a prestigious position, although the hours were longer and I doubt if the pay was much more, and it was not as steady.

I'm told many people considered Ah Ba a Chinatown "big shot." In the early 1900s, much of Chinatown had moved from Pioneer Square, near the Seattle waterfront, up to its present location along King Street. Along with the relocation came new capital projects. Ah Ba helped with the fundraising for our family association, the Gee How Oak Tin Association, which consists of families with the surnames Chan, Woo or Yuen. He also helped raise money for construction in 1929 of the Chong Wa Benevolent Association, the umbrella organization for all the Chinese associations and clubs in the region. The building still stands in Chinatown. My father coordinated visits by dignitaries to Chinatown, like Madam Chiang Kai-shek, who came to Seattle during World War II. I regret cutting up the souvenir program of Madam Chiang's Seattle visit for one of my elementary school book reports.

Ah Ba was the secretary of the China War Relief for the Chong Wa Benevolent Association. That meant he was Chinatown's main contact with city officials and anyone else outside of the area during the War. We rarely saw Ah Ba outside of the Don Ting Café where we took all our meals. After the restaurant closed at 2 a.m., he would stay at the restaurant to work on Chong Wa's business, which included translating, correspondence and accounting. He also managed Gee How Oak Tin Association's monthly loans to local merchants and residents.

5¢   SEATTLE, AUGUST 11, 1945   9

RATIONING T
SUGAR—Book 4, Stamp 36 valid throug
tember 1.
PROCESSED FOODS—Book 4, Blue Sta
through August 27; D-1, E-1, F-1, (
J-1, K-1, L-1, M-1, N-1 valid thro
T-1 valid through November 30.
MEAT, BUTTER, CHEESE, SHORTENIN
8-2, T-2, U-3 valid through Augus
through September 30; A-1, B-1, C-1
F-1, G-1, H-1, J-1, K-1 valid throu

GOOD NEWS TO CHINESE—Cleaver emphasizes feelings of Fong Dong, cook (left), as Chen P. Kan, proprietor of the Don Ting Cafe, 509 7th Ave S., shows him news of Japs' willingness to end war. Chen P. Kan also is secretary of China War Relief.

—(Post-Intelligencer Photo.)

Chan D. Kan (right) and Fong Dong. Posting notice of War's end. Seattle Post-Intelligencer, August 11, 1945.

At the time, it was very difficult for immigrants to get loans outside of Chinatown.

I adored Ah Ba. I would crawl up on his lap and give him a hug, which was atypical because, like most Chinese families, ours was not openly affectionate. Ah Ma and my older siblings kept a distance, but Ah Ba and I had a special bond. Once I colored all over our new wallpaper after we moved to our house on Jefferson Street. Ah Ma directed Ah Ba to punish me with a spanking. Behind closed doors, he only pretended to spank me soundly while I made the appropriate crying sounds.

I have a picture of him as a handsome young man playing the butterfly harp. But the Ah Ba I knew was a mature, chubby, well-dressed, teddy-bear of a man. He always wore freshly laundered dress shirts and a suit. At home, he took off his jacket and unbuttoned his shirt, but still kept his vest on. The only meal we ate outside of the restaurant was on Sundays. If Ah Ma cooked, it was steak and pork chops. I wanted only the bones of the pork chops along with lots of catsup. I love sweet red sauce. My favorite dish is tomato beef chow mein, which my *hapa haole* (part-Caucasian) Connecticut grandchildren also love. Ah Ba liked red sauce too. His favorite day-off activity was taking all of us to dinner at the fancy Italian Village restaurant and to see a movie at the Coliseum Theater on Fifth Avenue in downtown Seattle. After the movie, we would all go back home, except Ah Ba, who returned to the restaurant.

He loved the foods he was supposed to avoid, like fatty pork. That was what he ate on the day he had his heart attack in 1948. I remember the commotion that Monday morning as we were getting up for school. An ambulance came, and everyone was scurrying around. I

Ah Ba's funeral; John holding photo – The Seattle Times, March 18, 1948.

THIRD
MAIN NEWS
The

Twain Meet as Chinese Bury Revered Mr. Chin

--Times staff photo by Howard J. Vallentyne, Jr.
Left to right—MARY CHIN, JOHNNY WONG, JOHN FAY CHIN and HOWARD CHIN
Grieving son carried father's picture away from grave

asked what was going on. Someone told me to never mind, to just go to school. After school, no one was home, which wasn't all that unusual so when the bus came to take me to Chinese School, I went. Chinese School was held at Chong Wa from 5:00 to 7:00 p.m. during the week. That evening Mr. Eng from the China Cab came into our classroom and whispered something to the teacher, who gave me a peculiar look and gently told me to go with Mr. Eng. He said nothing to me in the cab. When we arrived at our home on Jefferson Street, every light was on and people were all around making lots of noise crying. Ah Ma was the loudest. I saw my Uncle Tommy and asked him to tell me what was happening. He told me, "*Nee ga ba gwah how* (Your father 'went over')." I thought he had told me that my father had gone away. I didn't understand that he meant that Ah Ba had died.

It wasn't until a couple days later when we visited Ah Ba at the old Bonney-Watson Funeral Home on Broadway and Spring Street that I knew what Uncle Tommy was trying to tell me. Ah Ba was embalmed and stayed in the mortuary until his funeral several weeks after his passing. We would visit him often. He looked like he was sleeping. Ah Ma would lay prone on the carpet, pound her fists and cry loudly, as if she hoped she could wake him up. It was embarrassing, but we didn't dare say anything. I didn't cry much because everything seemed so surreal and out of my control.

The reason for the delay in the service was to accommodate the Chinatown officials and guests from San Francisco and other Northwest cities. There is a Chinese custom that the funeral procession must travel past the family home before interment. Ah Ma rented enough black limousines for the dignitaries so that the cars stretched from our house on 15th and Jefferson all the way up the hill to Ruby Chow's restaurant on Broadway and Jefferson. The door to our house was left open so that Ah Ba's spirit could find its way home. The Seattle papers ran a photo of my brother, who was 11 at that time, leading the gravesite procession, carrying a portrait of Ah Ba followed by a traditional Chinese band. There was a

Chan family plot at Lakeview Cemetery.

banquet at Don Ting afterwards. It was then that I broke down because it seemed so inappropriate that everyone was socializing and having a party when my Ah Ba died.

It was my first funeral and one of the last of its kind. Ah Ba was interred at Lakeview Cemetery on a north slope facing 15th Avenue overlooking Lake Washington. The older Chinese section south of it was already filled. His was the first and the largest headstone on that slope. Ah Ma spent $4,000 for the funeral and headstone, a huge sum at that time, considering that our Central District home had only cost $2,000 two years earlier. But it was important for her to "save face" by spending the money necessary to mark Ah Ba's passing and to remember him as a respected community leader.

Ah Ma died 26 years later and was buried alongside him. There was little fanfare when she passed away. I remember how disappointed I was at the sparse attendance at her funeral. It could have been because we didn't know how to do a proper traditional Chinese send-off,

or it may have been because most of her friends had already passed on. Still I wished we could have done a little more for her. When we had Ah Ma's Chinese name, Ho Tim Sum, engraved on the tombstone, I thought it literally meant *Ho* (Good) *Tim* (Sweet) *Sum* (Heart). Perhaps she spent so much time on Ah Ba's marker because she knew that without him, she became a non-entity and someday she would be there, too. Recently, I visited the gravesite to find Ah Ma's family surname and village. The Chinese inscription only confirmed that Ah Ma was Chan D. Kan's wife.

In 1976, two years after Ah Ma passed away, my brother John died. He had never married and passed away one week after his 41th birthday. He was buried alongside my parents. He had Ah Ba's bad heart and the same penchant for eating the wrong things. We had Chinese banquets following the memorials for Ah Ma and for John, which were appropriate and healing. The three are together under that 1948 marker flanked by 20 foot high twin evergreens that Ah Ma and I planted as seedlings. It is still the largest marker on the slope.

Ah Ba may have been a big shot, but Ah Ma was the one with the tenacity.

Ho Tim Sum with Mari, 1936
– Author's photo.

I've heard my mother first immigrated to Seattle as a wet nurse of the granddaughter of one of Chinatown's most successful merchants, Chin Chun Hock, owner of Seattle's Quong Tuck Company. When she went through immigration as part of the family entourage, the story goes, the officials asked who she was. Chin said she was his servant and they promptly told him that America did not permit slavery. Mom became a free agent, and worked at Tuck Sing Company where she met and married Ah Ba within six months.

Ah Ma was 41 years old when I was born. She was considered pretty, but I remember her as older, unsmiling, 4'10", size 22 woman with a dowager's back, hair rolled in a net, wearing glasses. After Ah Ba died, she always dressed in black, except for special occasions. I suppose by then, there wasn't much to smile about. Ah Ma had left a spouse and children in China and had come to America as a servant in hopes of bringing them to "Gold Mountain." However, her family perished in China, either from famine or war. Then she managed to marry a Chinatown "big shot," only to be widowed and left in debt 13 years later with three children, aged 12, 11 and seven. I was the youngest one. There were days when at the end of day, the till was less than the $100 we put in before opening. I also shuddered whenever the cold weather came because often Ah Ma could not pay the utility bills.

Ah Ma was never affectionate, but showed her love in non-verbal ways. She would take me by bus to the Ice Capades and the Puyallup Fair. Her favorite entertainment though was wrestling matches at Eagles' Auditorium. She would save me the juicy ends of freshly roasted barbecue pork, or make my favorite tomato beef chow mein whenever I dropped into the restaurant. Everyone loved my birthday parties because of her crispy chicken marinated in bean curd, soy sauce and dusted with Swan's Down Cake Flour. It was the only chicken I would eat. She would come into my bedroom after closing the restaurant at 2 a.m. to cover my shoulders every night. Even today, I still need to cover my shoulders before falling asleep.

Ah Ma suffered a stroke in January 1964 after shopping and carrying two full bags of ingredients along with gallons of vinegar to make traditional dishes for our son's month-old party before going to work. She came to live with us until we could no longer care for her properly and had to move her to a nursing home. Today, we have the Kin On Nursing Home for Chinese-speaking elderly like Ah Ma, but back then, there was no Chinese nursing home for her to go to in Seattle. It was tough for someone who had never learned to speak English and ate nothing but Chinese food. She ran away from the nursing home once. It was amazing, considering she had totally lost her ability to speak by then and could not walk without a four-footed cane. Somehow, though, she managed to hail a yellow cab and direct the driver to take her to my Beacon Hill house. That's tenacity.

Fifty years after Ah Ba worked there, my architect husband Joey designed the plans to convert the old Quong Tuck Co. into a new space for the new Quong Tuck Restaurant. This was where Ah Ba had first worked when he came to Seattle many years earlier. Later, after the restaurant closed, that space became part of the new Wing Luke Asian Museum, which took over the entire building and renovated it into its new home in 2008.

Longtime community advocates Ben and Ruth Woo were our closest and dearest friends. Ben passed away in 2008. Ben Woo's first wife, Esther, was the granddaughter of Chin Chun Hock. She was the one whom my mother supposedly nursed after she had come to America. It seems we've come full circle in a very short time.

In the late 1800s, the U.S. government passed a series of laws excluding Chinese immigrant laborers and Chinese women. Because of these laws, America's Chinatowns were largely bachelor societies by the 1940s. Many of the men had wives and children in China who were unable to come to America. During my growing up years, there was a very small Chinese community in Seattle, numbering no more than about 5,000.

As we ABCs grew up in the 1950s, our lives were very carefree. We wore poodle skirts and crinolines and felt that we were no different from any other American teenagers. But for our immigrant parents, it was a cautious era. Only a few years had passed since the wartime hysteria that resulted in the removal of nearly all West Coast Japanese Americans

Vera at Garfield High School, 1956 – Author's photo.

to concentration camps. America's fear of communism and the Bamboo Curtain made the elders distrustful of their social and political situation as McCarthyism spread. Yet they found ways to send money back to their families in China who depended on the money for basic survival.

Those already in America with falsified immigration documents feared deportation. Because of this, America's Chinatowns of the 1950s were strongly anti-Communist and pro-Taiwan. The People's Republic of China wasn't officially recognized, so sending money to your relatives on the mainland was very clandestine and never talked about with the children. During the McCarthy era, elders were always afraid they would be considered communist sympathizers. That's why there was so much flag-waving for Taiwan and the Kuomintang Party. Every Chinatown went Kuomintang and I thought that was the only China. The other China, communist China, was something unknown. In retrospect, it's understandable why they didn't tell their ABC children much about their family backgrounds.

Because Chinatown was very pro-America, the mainstream papers portrayed the Chinese as the exotic model minority and community festivals were always covered in a positive light. I was often asked to be the one of the "cute little Chinese girls" helping with gala openings. One memorable event was the world premiere of the movie "Hong Kong" in 1952 at the newly renovated Chinese-themed Fifth Avenue Theater attended by the movie's stars Rhonda Fleming and Ronald Reagan. The good press we enjoyed was linked to the strong anti-Communist and pro-Taiwan sentiments of America's Chinatowns.

In the 1950s, a new type of leadership emerged to replace pioneers like my father. Every major Chinatown in the country seemed to have a restaurant with a dynamic woman owner who, with their elaborate hairdos, red lipstick, Chinese dress and no-nonsense personalities, contributed to the mystique of the Chinese community. Seattle had Ruby Chow. Her restaurant, "Ruby Chow's," like her counterparts' in other cities, mostly catered to the white community and were places where powerful and well-connected people met, including

Clockwise from top left: Ark Chin, Ruby Chow, Ben Woo, Wing Luke and Warren Chan – Wing Luke Asian Museum photo.

mayors, city council, state representatives and congressmen. In Ruby's place, deals were made, community events and festivals were planned, and political adversaries were trumped. These women, Ruby Chow in Seattle and Ruby Foo of San Francisco, really helped with the good press in the 1950s. But it also contributed to the stereotype of "dragon lady" and "exotic lady" because of how they looked, with their complicated upswept hairdos. They had good intentions and a deep commitment to the Chinese community as they knew it. But the Chinese community – which had previously been nearly all Toisanese-speaking – was starting to expand and become more diverse as immigrants from other parts of China and Southeast Asia began coming to America.

By the 1960s, the Civil Rights Movement had burst the homogeneous bubble of the white establishment and brought opportunities for upward mobility and acceptance for Asians. For many, it was the small crack of light they needed to be able to pursue and fulfill their Asian American dream. In 1965, the U.S. Congress passed major immigration reform legislation, dramatically increasing the number of slots available for immigrants from Asia. The liberalized laws allowed the Chinese community to grow. While earlier immigrants were peasants from the same poor regions in Guangdong Province, newer arrivals came from all walks of life from all over Asia, often with political affiliations that conflicted with the political beliefs of the earlier arrivals.

During the 1960s, Seattle was experiencing its own political reform movement. One of the champions of the "new wave" of government reform was a young Chinese American, Wing Luke, elected to the Seattle City Council in 1962. Wing was the first Asian American to win public office in the Pacific Northwest. He helped pass one of the first open housing ordinances in the nation, dismantling the system of restrictive covenants that barred Asians and other people of color from buying houses in many neighborhoods in Seattle. Tragically, Wing was never to enjoy his legacy. He perished in a plane crash in 1965. The plane was piloted by good friend and fair housing advocate Sid Gerber, and the accident took place shortly after passage of the Equal Housing Ordinance.

Before 1965, restrictive covenants and overt discrimination made it very difficult for

Asian Americans to move out of Chinatown and low-income neighborhoods. Asian American physicians who had the means to buy an upscale house in Bellevue were told, "Why don't you want to live with your own kind?" In the late 1950s, my sister and her Boeing engineer husband could not get anyone to sell them a home in the new Lake Hills development in Bellevue. When I was married in 1960 and my husband and I wanted to rent an apartment on the west side of Beacon Hill, the manager told us that the unit had just been rented. However, the vacancy sign remained on the building throughout the seven years we lived in the area.

By the 1950s, Seattle officially began referring to Chinatown as the "International Area," recognizing that it was the only neighborhood in the continental United States settled by Chinese, Japanese, Filipino and other ethnic groups living together. In the 1970s, the activists – many of whom were second and third generation Asians – were out in full force, taking charge and calling the area the "International District" because they embraced the vision of a more diverse community and wanted a more cooperative vision for the District. Community leaders like Bob Santos, Ben Woo, Tomio Moriguchi and Shigeko Uno became involved with the Model Cities program, procuring federal funds to rebuild urban neighborhoods, including the International District. They created the Seattle Chinatown-International District Preservation and Development Authority (SCIDPDA) to distribute funding for the rehabilitation of old buildings. The era of the 1970s was one of the first times in the United States that the different Asian groups in the same District were able to put aside their differences and work together.

However, some of the Chinatown leaders met this effort with resistance because they feared dilution of their identity and loss of their longtime access to city policymakers. Throughout the six months when Bob Santos, Barry Mar, Tomio Moriguchi, Shigeko Uno, Ben Woo and I were writing the SCIDPDA charter, Ruby Chow's supporters were writing a charter, too. Ruby was quick to use her celebrity status to lobby then Seattle Mayor Wes Uhlman and others on behalf of her "Chinatown" vision. As a compromise, Uhlman officially designated the area the Chinatown-International District. Yet despite this internal community tension, Seattle's Asian Pacific American community has emerged as a model for cooperation among different Asian American groups and a political force on the national stage. Positive change has happened without the different Asian Pacific Islander groups losing their individual identities.

During the 1980s, I wrote a column in Chinese American community papers throughout North America. It was titled "Dim Sum: Bits of the Asian American Dream." My goal for the column was to recall light-hearted experiences and traditions of second generation children of hard-working first generation immigrants. I wanted the column to reflect the Asian American dream, whether it was the dream of people whose sojourner fathers built the railroads during the 1860s, or whether it was the dream of my generation of ABCs, whose parents came at the turn of the century as merchants or students, or the dreams of educated families or political refugees who came after the 1960s, when immigration quotas were relaxed.

The desire to capture and share my own Asian American dreams became more important to me after I became a doting *Popo* (grandmother) of Connor and Carlyn Ing Dougherty and Trevor and Justine Hwang Ing.

Family history is an important part of your identity regardless of your background or whether you are Asian American or not. Our parents' Asian American dream was based on the shared aspiration of immigrants to give their children a better life – a better education and better job opportunities – and to instill in their children basic traditional values. For the immigrant generation, respect in the family and community means much more than what one earns or achieves as an individual.

Dim Sum
Bits of the Asian American Dream
By Vera Ing

Today's American dream seems to be based solely on financial and material success. How much one makes or has seems to be more important than anything else. But achieving happiness has nothing to do with financial success. Just look at the alcohol problems, divorce rates, drugs, graft and suicide stories among the affluent. Chasing the "new" American dream may be related to America's current discontent and divisions. Those who are not able to achieve their goals often are the first to blame it on inequalities. But discrimination is something that every group and every community has had to overcome. Staying connected is how to achieve your dreams in this country.

From left: Trevor Hwang Ing, Joey, Justine Hwang Ing, Vera, Connor Ing Dougherty, Carlyn Ing Dougherty – Author's photo.

Through their tenacity and resourcefulness, our first generation immigrant community survived and persevered, despite unthinkable hardships and discrimination. They laid the foundation for the success of their children and for the acceptance of Asian Americans into the broader society. Their ABC children have enjoyed opportunities and lifestyles they could never have imagined. By living through us, our parents have had the chance to fulfill their Asian American dream.

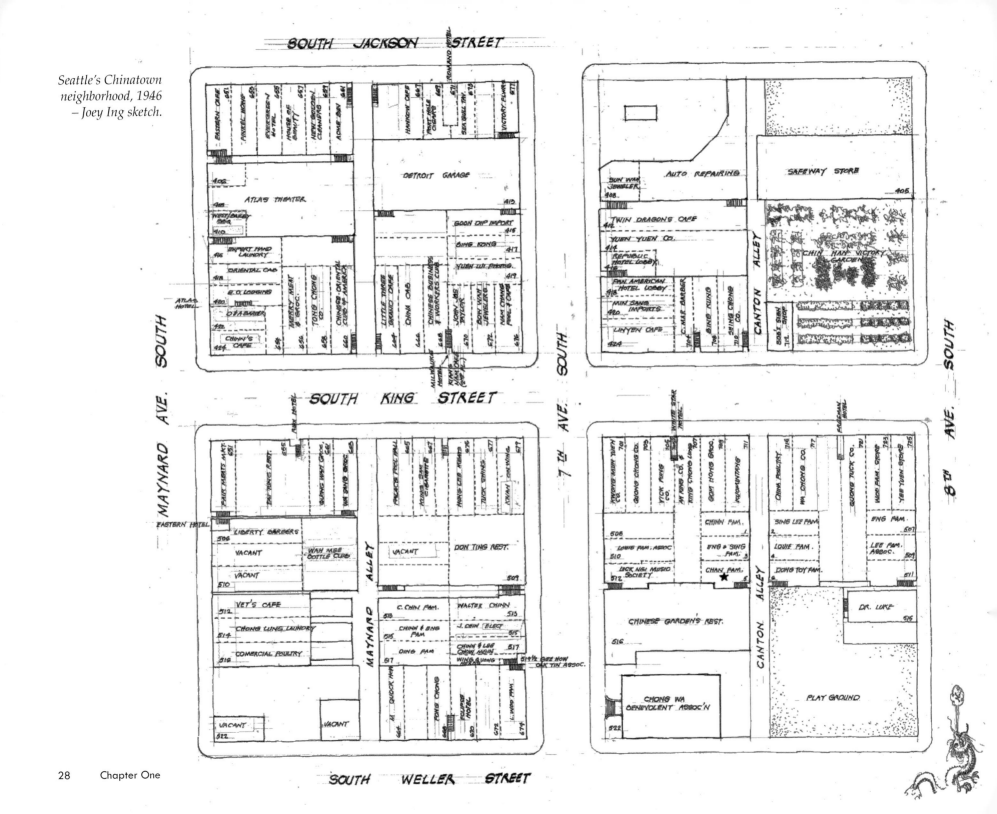

Seattle's Chinatown neighborhood, 1946 – Joey Ing sketch.

SOUTH JACKSON STREET

Top-left block (bounded by Maynard Ave South, South Jackson Street, 7th Ave South, South King Street):
EASTERN CAFE 651 · FINKEL HOME 653 · EVERGREEN HOTEL 655 · HOUSE OF BEAUTY 657 · NEW GARDEN CLEANERS 659 · ACME DRY 661
402 · ATLAS THEATER · 408 · WEST/BAILEY 390 · 410 · 416 EXPERT HAND LAUNDRY · ORIENTAL CAB 418 · E.O. LODGINGS 420 · O.F.A. BARBER · CHINN'S CAFE 424
MERRY MEAT GROC. 649 · TONG CHONG CO. 657 · CHINESE-ORIENTAL CLUB OF AMERICA 660
ROMANO HOTEL · HANROW CAFE · PORT HOLE CIGARS 645 · SEA GRILL TAV. 647 · 675 · VICTORY FLWRS 677
DETROIT GARAGE · 412
GOON DIP IMPORT 415 · BING KONG 417 · YUEN TUI PHOTO 419
LITTLE THREE GRAND CAFE · CHINA CAB · CHINESE BUSINESS & WORKERS CLUB 668 · JOHN JAS TAYLOR · BOY WAY JEWELERS · NAM CHANG POOL & CAFE 674
644 · 646 · 670 · 672 · 676
MILWAUKEE HOTEL · KIN'S NAM CAFE (2ND FL.)

Top-right block (bounded by 7th Ave South, South Jackson Street, Canton Alley, South King Street):
AUTO REPAIRING · SAFEWAY STORE
SUN WAH JEWELER 406 · TWIN DRAGONS CAFE 412 · YUEN YUEN CO. 414 · REPUBLIC HOTEL LOBBY 416 · PAN AMERICAN HOTEL LOBBY 418 · MIN SANG IMPORTS 420 · LIN YEN CAFE 424
405
CHIN HAY VICTORY GARDENS
CLMAR BARBER 704 · BING KUNG 708 · SHING CHONG CO. 710 · BOB'S SIGN SHOP 712

SOUTH KING STREET

Bottom-left block (bounded by Maynard Ave South, South King Street, Maynard Alley / 7th Ave South, South Weller Street):
PARK MEATS MKT. 651 · DAI TUNG REST. 655 · GUANG WAH GROC. 661 · WA SING GROC. 665
EASTERN HOTEL · LIBERTY BARBERS 506 · VACANT · VACANT 510 · VET'S CAFE 512 · CHONG LUNG LAUNDRY 514 · COMMERCIAL POULTRY 516 · VACANT 522
WAH MEE BOTTLE CLUB
PALACE PICK HALL 665 · KONG SAM CIGARETTE 667 · HANG LEE MEATS 676 · TUCK SHING 677 · KWAN CHU KING 677
VACANT · DON TING REST. 509
C. CHIN FAM. 513 · WALTER CHINN 513 · CHINN & SING FAM. 515 · J. CHIN ELECT · OING FAM. 517 · CHINN & LEE CHOW MEIN 517 · WING & WONG 519½ · OAK TIN ASSOC. SEE HOW
NEW HOTEL · VACANT 522 · VACANT
M. QUOCK HAM · TONG CHONG 664 · ECLIPSE HOTEL 670 · L. WOO FAM. 672 · 674

Bottom-right block (bounded by 7th Ave South, South King Street, Canton Alley, South Weller Street):
KWONG MULTI TRADY 700 · GUONG CHONG CO. 703 · YICK FUNG CO. · HI KING CO. · WHITE STAR HOTEL 705 · KING CHONG LUNG 707 · GOEY HONG GROC. 709 · KUOMINTANG 711
CHINA POULTRY 715 · WA CHONG CO. 717 · SUGHIE TUCK CO. 721 · 723 · YEE YUEN STORE 725
FREEMAN HOTEL
508 · CHINN FAM. · SING LEE FAM. · ENG FAM. 507
LOUIE FAM. ASSOC. 510 · ENG & SING FAM. · LOUIE FAM. · LEE FAM. ASSOC. 509
LICK NGI MUSIC SOCIETY 512 · CHAN FAM. ★ · DONG TOY FAM. · 511
CHINESE GARDEN'S REST. 516 · DR. LUKE 515
CHONG WA BENEVOLENT ASSOC'N 522 · PLAY GROUND

SOUTH WELLER STREET

Golden Years
Born Lucky in Seattle's International District

Golden Years

Born Lucky in Seattle's International District

The First Seven Years: Canton Alley

According to Chinese belief, bad luck is only temporary and cyclical. After five years of bad luck, seven years of good luck will follow. The pattern of seven good years, five bad years, seven good years mirrors the cycle of my own life.

I consider my first seven years a lucky time. I felt secure growing up in Chinatown. The next five years were not as good: my father passed away and my mother had a difficult time adjusting; life was not as carefree after I took on responsibility for an infant sister my mom had adopted. The next seven years were much happier, as I made life-long friends in junior and senior high school, then met and married Joey, my lifetime partner.

I was born into a pretty traditional Chinese American family. During my growing up years, my parents raised us with Confucian teachings. As children, we were taught to obey and not to question authority. We were taught the value of hard work, honesty and respect for elders and ancestors. We were warned not to bring shame upon the family. These values were drilled into us in the home.

As a family, we weren't especially religious, but Ah Ma did send us to Seattle Chinese Baptist Church. I attended Sunday services from the time I was very young. The church was located in Chinatown on 10th Avenue South and South King Street. Rev. Paul Fong was the minister, but none of us kids ever listened to what he was saying. As teenagers, all of us girls would pass notes back and forth between us while he was talking. I'm sure I didn't hear or learn much in church.

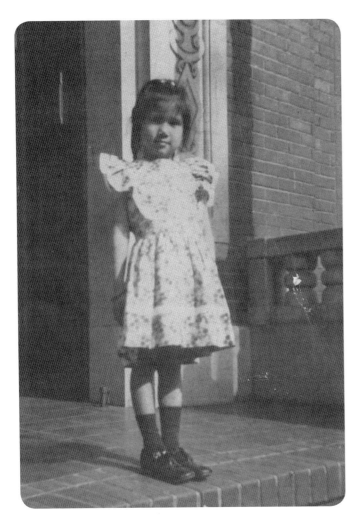

*Vera on Chong Wa steps. 1945
– Author's photo.*

Raised with Confucian values, Christian teachings and Chinese superstitions, I think I have an open attitude toward the beliefs of other people. Just as I am a unique mix of influences, others may have a different perspective and approach to a purposeful life. To me, that's okay. It's by meeting and getting to know others from different backgrounds that you grow as an individual. There is no single "right" viewpoint. There are many doctrines that teach that a person's fate is up to a higher power, that one's indiscretions must ultimately be accounted for, and that no matter how bad things get, there's always light at the end of the tunnel.

The ABC traditions and values are also heavily influenced by Chinese superstition and astrology. Lunar New Year is based on the movement of the Moon. As a result, the start of the Chinese New Year is different every year and starts between late January to the end of February. Each year of the twelve-year cycles is represented by an animal which represents individual characteristics as well as what to expect in the coming year.

I was born on September 28, 1940 in the lucky Year of the Dragon, on the birthday of Confucius. Chinese believe that having a child in the Year of the Dragon will bring good luck to the family. Because Chinese traditionally favor sons, my parents probably hoped that I would be a boy to bring them double luck. Unfortunately for them that wasn't the case. Still, they believed that I was a lucky child.

My parents left me in the hospital for a month. I'm guessing that they did this to make sure I survived the critical first few weeks and because it only cost a dollar a day to stay in the hospital back then. From the hospital, they brought me home to Canton Alley in Chinatown. My parents held a big "month-old" baby banquet to celebrate my birth at the fancy second-story Kiang Nam Restaurant in Chinatown, which later became the popular Art Louie Restaurant where Ah Ma worked after she sold the Don Ting Café.

As the name implies, Canton Alley is located in Chinatown. The Alley is off of South King Street, between Seventh and Eighth Avenues. It consisted

of a row of storefront apartments on both sides of the narrow lane between the East and West Kong Yick buildings, two hotels on north side of King Street. Canton Alley was occupied by Chinese families before World War II.

In that era, the restrictive housing covenants forced Asians to live in certain sections of the city – in Chinatown and the surrounding blocks. The Japanese lived up the hill on Main Street. The Filipino establishments – pool halls, cafes and shops – were on Maynard Avenue and throughout the District. Jackson Street, one block north of King Street, was the major traffic thoroughfare where we caught the bus. The core of Chinatown was four square blocks between King and Weller Streets and Seventh and Eighth Avenues.

Canton Alley had five apartments on each side. We lived in the last unit on the west side of the alley. The International District Emergency Center, run by medic Donnie Chin, occupied the Eng apartment below us for many years. Adjacent to the alley was the kitchen door of a restaurant, Chinese Garden, owned by the father of Art and George Louie. Today, the restaurant is called China Gate. The Chong Wa Benevolent Association, where I attended Chinese school, took up the rest of the block. There was a metal swing set in the side yard of Chong Wa. I would walk by the swings on my way to my parents' restaurant on Seventh Avenue, the Don Ting Café, which is now the Sea Garden Restaurant.

Our humble home in Canton Alley was a one-bedroom apartment. It was pretty crowded, but all the families in Chinatown lived that way. Ah Ma slept with my older siblings in one bed. Ah Ba had a bed behind a partition in the living room. I slept in a brown iron crib with railings; the crib also served as my playpen. I was told that once my mother and her mah jong group couldn't find me. Apparently, I had fallen out and had rolled under the crib and was hidden by things stored underneath. Ah Ma's long-time mah jong friend, Mrs. Mon Wai from Yakima, never tired of telling me that story so it must have been quite a comical scene.

Our apartment was upstairs, next to the Chinese Garden Restaurant. The smells of ginger, garlic and hot oil must have permeated our apartment because whenever I enter a Chinese restaurant, I am reminded of Canton Alley and the Don Ting. Below us were the Chinns. The adjacent two units housed the Engs and his brother, wife and nine children. One

Chinese Garden Restaurant, across from Don Ting, 1937 – Washington State Archives, Puget Sound Branch.

of the daughters, Charlene Eng Ko has been a lifelong friend. Another Chinn family lived on the other end of our side of the alley. Hannah was a friend of my sister Mari. Hopkin was my age. I ran into Hopkin at tai chi sessions outside the Beacon Hill Elementary School and at ballroom dancing classes at Yesler Terrace. Hopkin patiently helped me through the basics. It's easy to fall in step with childhood friends even if you haven't seen them for a long time.

Someone's grandfather had a carpentry shop on the other side of the alley, where we little kids played. The Louies lived in the middle unit; their son was my brother's playmate. The Dongs lived directly across the alley from us. Johnny Dong and his gang would climb to the roof of the Chinese school and shoot spit wads at "intruders." After he let me join them, I had a big crush on him. I was five and got to make the spit wads.

At ages nine and ten, my older siblings were responsible for taking care of me while my folks worked at the restaurant. We ate all our meals at the restaurant. After dinner, my big sister and brother would take me back to Canton Alley one block away. If I cried during the evening, Mari pretended to call our parents and say that Ah Ma told me to behave or she would be mad. We didn't have a phone, but this trick worked every time.

We all went to the nickel Saturday matinee movies at the Atlas Theater on Maynard Avenue and then for ice cream cones at the ice creamery owned by Shigeko and Chick Uno on Jackson Street. When it was John's turn to take care of me, we would go see the scary movies he liked. I would close my eyes and ask him to let me know when the scary part was over. He always told me to open my eyes at the goriest moment. I never learned and opened my eyes, despite knowing he was probably fooling me.

The Canton Alley neighbors and the King Street shopkeepers were our extended family, Florence Eng, matriarch of Wa Sang Grocery, which was located next door to the Tai Tung Restaurant on King Street, was particularly kind and always gave us an extra bag of treats whenever we "Chinatown brats" went to her store. As the eldest in the family, "Auntie" Florence – we called her auntie out of respect – took over the store after their father died in a car accident. She ran the store with her younger brothers Ray, Byron and Winston. The family owned the building and also had businesses in Bremerton and the University District. My husband's sister worked in their University District gift store. I met my future husband at the wedding of Florence's daughter. Her brother Byron was in our wedding party. My architect husband Joey designed their drive-in restaurant in the University District and the Rex Apartments on King Street. Joey served on the first International Special Review District Board along with her brother Ray. Auntie Florence's son Darrel married Linda, a student I once tutored. Our interconnections were typical of the relationships that emerge in a small community like Chinatown.

If I was roaming around King Street at dusk, Auntie Florence would tell me to go home or she would call my mom. I was one of the more assertive Chinatown kids. Her son Donald had a jointed wooden crocodile that moved like a shimmering slinky dragon. I didn't want to give it back and told him that I was taking it to Mr. Chinn's carpentry shop so we could all play with it. Donald never asked for it back.

I will always remember the Christmas Ah Ma took me to see Santa Claus at the Frederick & Nelson department store in downtown Seattle. In those days, Frederick & Nelson was considered the premier high-end retailer in Seattle. It was always a dress-up affair for us, whether it was going to see Santa or putting on white gloves and our best dress for tea in their basement restaurant on Mother's Day. Ah Ma spent extra time braiding my hair and dressed me in my brown teddy bear coat with the red collar where she pinned my "China" button. I asked Santa for a horse.

On Christmas Day, Ah Ba blindfolded me in his office above the restaurant and led me down the stairs. When I pulled off his handkerchief, I saw a wooden rocking horse so tall that I had to use a chair to get on it. It had button eyes, a black-and-white checkered cloth covering over its barreled body, and leatherette ears and tail. Okay, it wasn't the real horse that I wanted, but it was the closest I had gotten to getting what I asked for. It was the best childhood Christmas I can remember.

During the War, President Roosevelt encouraged everyone to start "victory gardens" and grow their own vegetables. Mrs. Chin Han's victory garden was on 8th and King Street where the Four Seas Restaurant is now. We ran through her garden on our way to the Jackson Street Safeway store (now the House of Hong Restaurant) to trade in our ration stamps for Wonder Bread, milk and – for special dinners – a tin of corned beef. Mr. Chin Han was at least 10 years younger than Ah Ba, but they worked together as colleagues in the family association and the Chong Wa Benevolent Association.

We Chinatown brats never ventured far from King Street. It was our entire universe. When we went out to play, we wore "China" buttons during the War because our parents feared that we would be taken away to internment camps like our Japanese American neighbors. I never saw a Japanese until first grade and was told that every overseas Chinese had lost at least one family member in China during the Japanese occupation. I imagined them as scary enemies and mapped out hiding places in Chinatown should they attack us.

One of my new friends in first grade was Janet Kudo. By that time, we had moved to the Central Area. We went to her house after school to play before the Chinese school bus picked me up at 4 o'clock. Unlike my mother, her mother was young and contemporary. I was surprised when Jan told me that she was Japanese. She didn't look anything like the comic book portrayals of Japanese and didn't fit the image of an enemy. She and her Japanese American parents looked like us and were more Americanized than our own Chinese parents. It was quite an epiphany.

I was never afraid being in Chinatown. I always felt my community "uncles" would come running out of the storefronts and family associations to protect me if anyone tried to cause me harm. My sister Mari told me that once after a Saturday matinee, there was a big seedy fellow who followed her out of the theater, but that she saw one of the "uncles," a much smaller man, keeping an eye on the situation and walking behind her until she got home safely.

The only family holidays we had took place when Ah Ba traveled to San Francisco to serve as a delegate at one of the Chinese association national conventions. On these occasions, he would take all of us with him. We would also get new clothes to wear. One year I got a white rabbit coat with a matching hat and muff. Once, Ah Ba hired a driver from Chinatown to take us to San Francisco in his brand new black Ford. The driver reminded me of Fred Astaire, with his impeccable three-piece suit, spats on his shoes and jaunty cane hat.

The year before my father's death, we went to San Francisco by train. We had our own sleeper compartment. As usual, Ah Ma bought Mari and I new coats and shoes to wear with our Chinese dresses that year. Mine was the prettiest rose color with pearl buttons and crisp new fabric. John got a new sport jacket and hat. He wore the same jacket and hat at Ah Ba's funeral. My coat had lost its finish and buttons by then. Ah Ma bought us a box of "Tiddly Winks" to occupy our time. I remember how the colorful plastic disks reflected the sunlight as we flipped them into the target on the moving train. My passion for glass art probably

Top: Chan family in San Francisco, 1947.
Bottom: Vera and Ah Ma in San Francisco, 1963 – Author's photos.

originated from that trip. We ate in the dining car and as usual I was going to order the cheapest meal. But Ah Ma told me to order up because it was "bad face" to act frugal when you were on vacation. I had my favorite meal, canned fruit cocktail, veal cutlet, applesauce, corn, mashed potatoes with gravy and ice cream. The San Francisco trips with Ah Ba were the only times we traveled in such grand style.

But my first seven years of good luck was coming to an end. Canton Alley was pretty humble living, but I cannot remember feeling deprived, envious or scared. We enjoyed the prestige of being Chan D. Kan's family. It does takes a village to raise a child. We were lucky during my first seven years to live in a place where everyone watched over us.

The Next Five Years: Jefferson Street

After the War, many Chinese Americans moved outside of Chinatown into neighborhoods like Beacon Hill and the Central Area. We moved to the Central Area. Because my parents were not citizens, our family homes were listed under my ABC brother's name even though he was under 10. My father bought a duplex off of 12th Avenue and Alder Street for $2,000. Uncle Tommy and Auntie So lived here, along with Dick and Annie Ko.

My mother bought a house on Jefferson for about the same price. We went to live at 1503 East Jefferson Street. It was huge compared to Canton Alley, but it soon became untidy and cluttered because Chinese people hate to throw anything away. The East Jefferson house had four stories, counting the attic, where Ah Ba slept, and a basement which had a coal furnace. There were four bedrooms on the second floor and one shared bathroom. The entry room had a built-in bench, which became a catch-all for our coats, packages and a little bit of everything. It housed the piano and Ah Ba's easy chair, next to the black rotary telephone.

SQUIRE PK. B-12. L-5.

1503 East Jefferson Street – Washington State Archives, Puget Sound Branch.

Our living room entrance had heavy oak sliding doors that never closed properly. A portrait of Ah Ba and Ah Ba's first wife (*Da Ma*) hung over the big radio console in a place of honor, along with a picture of President Franklin Roosevelt. During that era, Chinese American families saw Roosevelt as the savior of their families back in China during the Japanese occupation. On Chinese New Year, the console would be filled with a whole boiled chicken, oranges, and traditional New Year sweets like watermelon seeds, candied coconut and tins of Almond Roca.

On the fireplace mantle were Ah Ma's best set of vases, a laughing Buddha, an antique black granite clock with gold trim, and twin proverbs by Ah Ba about not talking without thinking. In the corner was Ah Ba's tall secretary desk, the front filled with pasted newspaper articles and snapshots. One was of a Chinese dragon dancing in front of Don Ting on V-E Day – May 8, 1945 – the day when the U.S. and the Allies announced the surrender of German forces in Europe. A client of my husband who was a property owner of many of the older buildings around town said Ah Ba kept the restaurant open all night when they heard of the victory. There were clippings of me dressed in the same green silk Chinese pajamas. In one, I was carrying a lantern in the Chinatown parade, another was with Charlene Woo, opening the Chinese section of the cemetery on Aurora, and another was at the reopening of the Fifth Avenue Theater with Rhonda Fleming and Ronald Reagan. One article was of John carrying Ah Ba's picture at his funeral.

Vera doing the dishes, 1949
– Author's photo.

The walls of our living room were hung with large portraits of departed relatives. The portraits would scare some of my friends, but to us they were just part of the room. There were no pictures of Ah Ma or us in the living room. In my mother's bedroom there was a group picture of 10 unsmiling young people, which Ah Ma told me were her "China children." Ah Ma was as silent as that picture about the specifics of this "family," so we never inquired further. I had assumed that it was because they had perished during the War and that it was too painful for her to tell us about it. But to this day, I still don't know exactly who those people were. I never got the full story.

The dining room of our East Jefferson home had a wall of windows facing our next door neighbors, the Chinns. We had a corner glass breakfront where Ah Ma displayed all her good Chinese dishes. We used the dining table as a makeshift ping pong table and used books as the "net" and 78 rpm records as paddles. The buffet was piled high with our schoolbooks. The three walls had ledge molding, which acted as display shelves filled with Ah Ma's artifacts, many purchased at the thrift stores.

The dining room had a swing door leading to the pantry and an unheated half-bath that no one used. The kitchen sink, where we washed dishes, was in the pantry. The pantry had built-in glass cabinets filled with Chinese dried herbs, medicine and delicacies we never ate, like the jars of dried beetles. We ate in the kitchen on a green and chrome Formica table. There was a potbelly stove and an electric stove next to the basement stairs. The back porch was enclosed and held an ice box before we got a refrigerator. In our fenced backyard were Ah Ma's garden of Chinese vegetables, fruit trees and a hedge of some kind. She would pick leaves off the hedge to make delicious soup, but I don't know what kind of plant it was. I've looked for those leaves in the Asian markets, but to this day, I'm still not sure what it was. We also had a garage, but no one could get into it because it was storage for Ah Ma's cast-offs.

Ah Ma slept in the second-story middle bedroom in front of the attic stairs, Mari and John had the two front bedrooms. I had the small back bedroom next to the bathroom. Ah Ba took the entire three-room attic for himself. My father and mother never shared a room, probably because Ah Ba always came home very late. The unfinished basement housed our coal bins and furnace. There were also clotheslines hung with Ah Ma's smelly *hom yee* (salted fish), a pantry with dusty canned peaches, laundry tubs and a wringer washer. Once my hand got caught in the wringer and I was rushed to the doctor. When we got home, she took off the clean bandages and rubbed my hand with Chinese medicine. It hurt like the dickens, but the wound did get better pretty fast after that.

After my father's death, Ah Ma moved to the large front bedroom and John moved up to the attic. The middle room was left vacant. Ah Ma filled the room where my father had his heart attack with all of Ah Ba's belongings. Ah Ma wore only black from then on and spent most of her time at the restaurant or playing mah jong. She was usually asleep in her locked bedroom by the time we got up for school. We children continued to look after ourselves, but without the help of a nearby Chinatown extended family.

A New Sister

When I was growing up, adoption, or as they call it in Hawaii, "hanai," within the community was very causal. My mother adopted my younger sister Helen in 1949, one year after my father died. At the time, Helen was just an infant. Ah Ma brought Helen home from the hospital without first telling us. I think she acted on some Chinese superstition or on her fear of not having anyone take care of her in her old age. Whatever the reasons, she did not change her schedule and I became Helen's surrogate mother at the tender age of 10. At the time, my older siblings were

Vera and John, 1950 — Author's photo.

already involved in teen activities. We were children raising children. Once I stayed home from school because Helen was sick. When the school office called, I hung up and ran out of the house with my baby sister because I was afraid the truant officers would come after us and take us both away.

The Jefferson Street neighbors were friendly, but they didn't look after us like the Chinese neighbors who made up the tight-knit Canton Alley community. A Japanese family lived on the corner. The father had a brand new 1949 forest green Ford and spent every Saturday washing and waxing it. On the other side of our house were the Chinns, with adult children Bertha, Wally and others. (The Chinns were the grandparents of Gloria Lung Wakayama, an attorney and long-time community leader.) Whenever she was baking, Mrs. Chinn would make one big cookie for me and Helen. Lee's Grocery was at the top of our block. Paul "Pee Wee" Lee was Helen's best friend in grade school. The sons later took over their father's Chinatown store, the Wah Young Company, an import-export store, formerly located in the East Kong Yick Building, which has now become the Wing Luke Asian Museum.

Across the street was Tak's Grocery. Tak, his wife and five daughters lived upstairs. Tak would open a new package of hot dogs and let me buy one for a nickel for Helen's dinner. Dinner was usually Campbell's vegetable soup with rice, which I heated up and cooked with a Chinese sausage or salted fish on top. A hot dog was a treat. So was fried egg sandwich with lots of catsup.

Next to Tak's was the all-female Yuen household. Their house had peeling paint, but they had the prettiest garden: sweet peas and sugar peas growing on strings across a dilapidated fence. The Dongs lived next to them – Donald was my age and also went to T.T. Minor Elementary School on 19th and East Union. My brother John had a crush on the pretty Filipino teen who lived on the corner. He found out early that girls liked to have their pictures taken. She posed for him in her hula skirt.

Everyone sat on the front porch in those days and we would shout at each other across the street. When the cool Filipino boys like Bob Santos walked down the street, Ah Ma would yell at me in Chinese to get back in the house. *"Vee-la, loy coy la!!"* We lived in a big house, and we yelled at lot at each other. She would also play Chinese opera music so loud on the wind-up record player that I could hear it at the top of the hill. There is a Chinese superstition that to frighten away spirits you stomp and shout and make noise. Whatever the reasons, ours was always a loud household.

I attended T.T. Minor Elementary School. My teachers were all unmarried white females with gray or white hair who smelled like cold cream and lavender. They were all very kind. My favorite teacher was Miss Noble. She taught me how to tell time properly. We made buttermilk once in class, something I had never tasted before. It was delicious.

Best of all, she took us to the Frye Art Museum on Boren Avenue. She told us it was free. To me, it was a wonderful new accessible world. Throughout childhood, the Frye was my special place. My favorite piece of art there is the Koester painting of fluffy ducks. I owe my lifelong appreciation of the arts to Miss Noble.

When I was attending elementary school, there were few Chinese going to T.T. Minor. I maintained my ABC friends from Chinese Baptist Church and Chinese school, where I still went after school every day. Pauline Woo – Bo Ling was her Chinese name – lived only two blocks south of me on Fir Street, but she attended Bailey Gatzert Elementary School. While our mothers played mah jong at her house, we children played canasta until *siu yeh* (midnight snack), then I would run home late at night. With all the dangerous people running around outside these days, I can't imagine staying out that late anymore.

My best grade school friends were Joanne and Virginia Chinn who lived on Beacon Hill. They were related to the Chin Han family. Joanne's mother didn't work at the store like

Central Area friends in front of the Woo house, 1946 – Author's photo.

Ah Ma and their house was like a second home to many of us. I would walk to their house every Saturday. My route took me from Jefferson south down 15th Avenue through Collins Playfield to Japanese Buddhist Church on Main Street. From there, I went west down Jackson Street past the Japanese produce stands to the Jewish Ten Cent Store on 12th Avenue. I would turn south past the Black & Tan Club across the street from Jan Kudo's father's gas station and past Bailey Gatzert Elementary School (where I went to kindergarten) to the 12th Avenue Bridge. I would trudge up the hill past the Marine Hospital and then eight more blocks to Joanne's house on 12th Avenue South.

On Sundays, I would walk past the Garland Florist shop on Jackson Street to go to Chinese Baptist Church on 10th and King. On Mother's Day, I would stop in the shop to buy a $1.00 corsage for Ah Ma to pin it on her apron while she cooked at Don Ting. When we became teens, we would go bowling after church at Main Street Bowl above Roma Café in the Takahashi Building. In 1971, Joey's architectural office moved into the vacant Roma Café space.

Ah Ma sold our restaurant in 1960 soon after I got married. Uncle Tommy went to work at Fisherman's Terminal on Elliott Avenue. Uncle Harry found a job at the fancy Trader Vic's Restaurant in downtown Seattle. Wong-Suk, our cook, and Ah Ma went to work at the popular Art Louie's Restaurant in Chinatown. He later worked at George and Rose Louie's Cuisine of China in Ballard. This was probably a much better situation for all three of them. I'm guessing that they each made more money, worked shorter hours, and had better benefits than they would have if they had continued at the Don Ting Café.

Like many Chinese Americans, Uncle Tommy, a World War II veteran, was finally able to bring his wife and children over after the War. They had a daughter Sue, who was my age, and a son, Eugene, who was about Helen's age. They first lived at our duplex on 12th Avenue and East Alder. They later moved to Yesler Terrace and then to a house near the Beacon Avenue junction. After Ah Ma had a stroke, Uncle Tommy and Uncle Harry, our closest "relatives," would invite us over to their homes where their wives would prepare special foods for Chinese holiday celebrations.

As a young mother, I loved going to Auntie So's Beacon Hill house during the Chinese holidays. She would make *doong tai*, a traditional favorite prepared during the Dragon Boat Festival, celebrated on the fifth day of the fifth month of the Chinese calendar. She always offered to teach me how to make those sticky sweet rice bundles wrapped in ti leaves. I did buy a package of ti leaves once and had planned to take her up on her invitation, but never did because our life was getting so full. I learned of her passing after the fact because I was out of town. It was years later before I threw out that dry package of leaves.

Auntie Lucy and Uncle Harry adopted two children around Helen's age. They often invited Helen over to their place to spend time or to go to church with them. Years later, Auntie Lucy and Uncle Harry came to our home for our first grandson's month-old party. By then, Uncle Harry was very frail so I set up a table on the front yard for them, thinking it would be too hard on him to walk up the steps to our house and maneuver around the 100 people inside. Now I wonder if he might have thought that I didn't want him to go inside. I should have found a way to bring Uncle Harry inside the house so that he could see the full fruits of his generosity and how appreciative I was for everything he and Uncle Tommy had done for us after Ah Ba had died.

The Next Seven Years: Junior and Senior High

During junior high school, church took the place of my extended Canton Alley family. Like most of my friends, I went to church for social reasons. While my ABC friends went only to Chinese Baptist Church (CBC), I went to several Asian American churches.

In elementary school, I signed up for Maryknoll summer school on 16th and Jefferson

Donald Kinsley's music class at Washington Junior High School, 1954 – Author's photo.

with my Filipino classmates because the nuns fed us lunch. On holidays, I would still go to Chinese Baptist Church with Joanne and Virginia, but I felt more comfortable in the Japanese community churches. In junior high, I went to Japanese Baptist Church up near Yesler Terrace because, unlike Chinese Baptist, JBC had sports and teen parties. I was in a trio with Amy Sanbo and Lorita Delma and sang on the radio broadcast of "Youth for Christ" every Saturday night at Seattle Pacific. I went to the teen dances at St. Peter's Episcopal Church on King Street. At Japanese Buddhist Church, on 14th Avenue and South Main Street, I watched the boys play basketball games and was one of the "groupies" who followed the "Skyliners," a Japanese American high school dance band, led by our Washington Junior High School Music Teacher Donald Kinsley.

The minister at Japanese Baptist Church was Rev. Emory Andrews, who followed his Japanese American congregation members to internment camp during World War II. Many years later, he married Joey and I. His advice to us as newlyweds was that when we started a family, we should bring our children to church because that is where they would forge friendships and experience first love. Rev. Andy was right. My first dates and lifelong friends were individuals I met at church.

We sent our three children to Chinese Baptist Church with our Mt. Baker neighbors Bruce and Delores Dong. CBC's Sunday school teachers included Diane Wong and Gary Locke, who later became Washington State Governor. Church playmates included Karen

The Skyliners' Garfield Funfest Act, 1956 – Author's photo.

Chinn, who worked at the *International Examiner* and married Philip Lee, co-founder of Lee & Low Books. Our son Joel became close friends with Karen and her husband years later when they were all working in New York. Every summer, they spent a week in Burien at Joey's sister's house, attending summer Bible camp. The three kids loved going to Auntie Bebe's because she always had food we rarely had at home like packaged snacks, candy, potato chips, pizza and her famous carrot cake.

Soon I was a budding teenager and going out on dates. At Washington Jr. High, I reconnected with Janet Kudo, who moved from the T.T. Minor area in the second grade. Other friends included Lorita Delma, Linda Maekawa, Janet Sakamoto, Kay Hirai, Lily Nakata and Amy Sanbo. We were in the same classes, played in the school orchestra, sang in chorus, and dated members of Skyliners Dance Band. We had our parties at my house because most of my Japanese American friends lived in apartments, Ah Ma was never around and it provided an opportunity for me to have fun at home at the same time I took care of my younger sister Helen, who was usually asleep upstairs.

Unlike some ABC parents who harbored World War II resentments against the Japanese, Ah Ma did not disapprove of my dating Japanese American boys, although she did warn me, "If you marry a Japanese, you will be expected to serve your husband!" My brother John's friends were all Japanese Americans who had been in the "Continental Dance Band," the forerunner to the Skyliners. I sang in John's band at Chinatown Night, which was part of the city-wide Seafair Festival.

Ah Ma was more demonstrative and opinionated about my ABC boyfriends. It was very evident if she disapproved of one of them. She scratched out the face of one from all the photos I had of him. Another time she symbolically used the broom to "sweep out" another. Once, she tried to fix me up with a rich Hong Kong student who ate daily at the Don Ting. I stopped being nice to the Hong Kong student when I saw him at the restaurant. None of her actions swayed me. I would have broken off with the boys she disliked sooner or been nicer to the student if she hadn't tried to force the issue.

Except for Chinese New Year, we never celebrated holidays at home. On Thanksgiving Day, I would take Helen to Mari's in-laws on 20th and Jackson and walk home because usually someone would come over and bring me a plate of turkey after their family dinner. On Christmas Eve, I would come home with my date, play carols on the record player and wake up Helen to open presents.

The only boyfriend Helen liked was Joey. They were both born under the same lunar sign, which according to Chinese astrology is very compatible with my sign. They also shared similar backgrounds. Joey also was the youngest in his family and had been on his own since losing his father at 10 and mother at 16. He got in trouble for youthful pranks like breaking into the school cafeteria and eating a pan of jello. Born in Honolulu, he had no higher aspirations than to work at Pearl Harbor like his older brothers until his high school shop teacher recognized his drafting skill and encouraged him to consider going into architecture. He came to school in Seattle because his sister Bebe lived in the area. Bebe worked for the Chinns in the University District. We met at Florence Eng's daughter's wedding in the summer following my high school graduation.

I liked Joey because he was the most atypical Chinese boy I dated. Instead of the usual movie and snack afterwards at "Clark's Around the Clock" Restaurant on Boren Street, we went to foreign films, University of Washington plays, parties where everyone wasn't Asian, and ate at Japanese restaurants. Our weekends were spent driving around the city in his battered 1949 Chevrolet to attend architectural exhibits and see new well-designed buildings located around the city. We chose to marry at the University Unitarian Church on 95th Avenue Northeast because architect Paul Hayden Kirk had won an American Institute of Architects design award for doing it.

Ah Ma liked him because he was Chinese. It was Joey who now got the juicy ends of the barbecued pork and favorite dishes at the restaurant. Although we hardly knew the wedding couple, Joey and I were asked to be in the wedding party of Uncle Tommy's daughter,

Sue. She and her husband's parents had arranged their meeting and marriage. At the reception, Mari asked Joey what his intentions were while I was away from the table. With all of the Chinese "relatives" at the table listening intently, Joey answered: "Dishonorable!" We both had a big laugh over how the family was so transparent in trying to get us together.

Joey asked me to marry him after he had graduated from the University of Washington with a degree in architecture and finished his six-month armed services obligation in the National Guard. I was 19 years old and Helen was 10. Ah Ma and Mari were ecstatic, and Helen cried when she found out.

Ah Ma took me to the family association where an elder determined the best day to marry and recorded both of our names in the village book. Joey didn't know his Chinese name and had to ask his oldest brother Noble in Honolulu to find it. When Noble sent it over, Ah Ma told me that Joey's family name was really Inn/Yen/Yuen not Ing/Eng/Ng like my sister's husband. It was a good thing it wasn't Chinn/Chan/Chun because it was taboo to marry someone with the same surname.

On the night before our wedding, Ah Ma was having her usual mah jong game. I heard Mrs. Mon Wai ask Ah Ma what she thought of Joey. Between the "dok" sounds of the tiles in play, she replied in Chinese: "He's poor, but he's a good boy! And ... he's an architect!" All the ladies exclaimed with approval, "Oooh!"

One year later, when we bought our first home in Beacon Hill on 24th Avenue South

Vera & Joey, wedding day, July 1960
– Author's photo.

*Vera, Helen, Mari, 1978
– Author's photo.*

across the street from the 11th hole of the Jefferson Park Golf Course, Helen moved in with us. Two years later, Ah Ma moved in, too. Helen was a big help to our growing family, growing into a beautiful woman. But she always seemed to be searching for something. In retrospect, I think Helen did not have the sense of belonging that Mari and I enjoyed growing up in Chinatown as Chan D. Kan's children. Helen was a song leader at Franklin High School and became a TWA stewardess at 19. She married her high school sweetheart and had two children. But she still felt that something was missing in her life. She repressed her feelings and went through a bad period that broke up her own family.

Church was the salvation for Helen. There, she found her faith, spiritual strength and acceptance in another community. She is the peacemaker between us three sisters. Throughout my life, I could always depend on her love. She is now married to Mason, brother of my T.T. Minor classmate, Seattle Community College District Chancellor Charles Mitchell, who shares her interests in art and sports. Helen has become a doting grandmother, and is at peace with herself. The right church had a lot to do with this.

In the summer of 2007, we had a dinner at our house for Shigeko Uno, a beloved International District icon and favorite colleague of mine. Other invited guests included I.D. movers and shakers of the 1970s like Ben Woo, Bob Santos, Tomio Moriguchi and Alan Kurimura. Shigeko, 92 at the time, was a beloved role model to me because she had more spunk than friends my own age. We served together for over 25 years on the board of the International District Improvement Association and Seattle Chinatown-International District Preservation and Development Authority. I always appreciated her because she was to me a community mother among a group of mostly men.

The best part of serving on these boards was having the chance to hang out with her and other I.D. movers and shakers afterwards. Shigeko smoked and drank her scotch neat, and more often than not, bought the first round. Shigeko and I and others like Ben Woo, Bob Santos, Alan Kurimura

Dinner at Tomio Moriguchi's home, 1995. 1st row, from left: Alan Kurimura, Christine Yurose Smith. 2nd row, from left: Dick Smith, Vera, Joey, Tomio Moriguchi, Shigeko Uno, Ruth Woo, Arlene Oki – Author's photo.

and Tomio Moriguchi would go to the Bush Garden and have drinks and snacks after our community meetings.

Shigeko is someone who always faced challenges with grace. Her family lost their dairy farm when they were forced, like other Japanese Americans, to abandon their homes and businesses during World War II. After the War, she and her husband Chick opened an ice creamery between 8th and 7th Avenues on Jackson Street. It was a favorite stop for all of us International District kids. Later, after she and her husband closed the ice cream store, she went to work as the bookkeeper for the Rainier Heat and Power Co., the major land holding company in the International District. As a result, she was instrumental in brokering the sale of several key properties back to the community for redevelopment.

In her later years, Shigeko still smoked and had her usual scotch. But by that time, she was quite frail. Once, she wanted to go to the backyard for a cigarette and join the other dinner guests there. To get there, though, she would have to go down a narrow spiral staircase.

My first reaction was to discourage her, then I remembered the time when she swam with me in our unheated pool on a cloudy Hydroplane Race Day party when she was over 65. I thought to myself, "If she wants walk down the staircase, we need to make it happen." We helped her get down. In part, I did this to make up for thinking my Uncle Harry was too frail to be in the middle of our grandson's month-old party.

Although Shigeko wasn't feeling her best at the dinner, her spirit was intact. She faced her last challenge with grace. During her last months, she continued her life as usual. On her good days, she went to meet her friends at Yummy Bakery in the I.D. We saw her with her daughter Debbie at the

Seattle International Film Festival at the viewing of a documentary on the Japanese American internment. She went on the annual memorial pilgrimage to Minidoka, Idaho, where most Japanese Americans from Seattle were incarcerated during World War II, and would join Bob Santos at the Bush Garden, the community watering hole, for drinks. Five weeks after our dinner, she passed on.

Even though Shigeko and I came from very different backgrounds, I feel fortunate in having had the opportunity to work in the community with her and get to know her. You cannot find a better example of a purposeful life.

Each one of us is unique, shaped by our ethnic values, religious faith and our encounters in school, at work and in our neighborhoods. As we make this journey through life, I believe that openness to different teachings and experiences makes one more trusting, tolerant and tranquil. We meet people who touch and change our lives. Instead of living in fear, we should try to learn from others, having faith that there is a higher power and there will always be light at the end of the tunnel. Remember that for every five years of bad luck, you'll experience seven good years. I know that is true because that's what has happened in my own life.

Animal Profiles

RAT: charming, charismatic, active, intuitive, lucky

OX: honest, solid, practical, steadfast, down to earth

TIGER: courageous, passionate, enthusiastic, optimistic

RABBIT: imaginative, sensitive, artistic, fussy, wise

DRAGON: dynamic, lucky, original, confident, popular

SNAKE: subtle, shrewd, perspicacious, stylish, proud

HORSE: busy, volatile, witty, vivacious, independent

SHEEP: arty, cultured, gentle, loving,

MONKEY: ingenious, intelligent, versatile, quick-witted

ROOSTER: passionate, focused, industrious, tidy

DOG: reliable, caring, honest, devoted, unselfish

PIG: sincere, gregarious, generous

The Chinese New Year Chart

1940 2/8/40 - 1/26/41 Dragon	**1958** 2/18/58 - 2/7/59 Dog	**1976** 1/31/76 - 2/17/77 Dragon	**1994** 2/10/94 - 1/30/95 Dog
1941 1/27/41- 2/14/42 Snake	**1959** 2/8/59 - 1/27/60 Pig	**1977** 2/18/77 - 2/6/78 Snake	**1995** 1/31/95 - 2/18/96 Pig
1942 2/15/42 - 2/4/43 Horse	**1960** 1/28/60 - 2/14/61 Rat	**1978** 2/7/78 - 1/27/79 Horse	**1996** 2/19/96 - 2/6/97 Rat
1943 2/5/43 - 1/24/44 Ram	**1961** 2/15/61 - 2/4/62 Ox	**1979** 1/28/79 - 2/15/80 Ram	**1997** 2/7/97 - 1/27/98 Ox
1944 1/25/44 - 2/12/45 Monkey	**1962** 2/5/62 - 1/24/63 Tiger	**1980** 2/16/80 - 2/4/81 Monkey	**1998** 1/28/98 - 2/15/99 Tiger
1945 2/13/45 - 2/1/46 Rooster	**1963** 1/25/63 - 2/12/64 Rabbit	**1981** 2/5/81 - 1/24/82 Rooster	**1999** 2/16/99 - 2/4/00 Rabbit
1946 2/2/46 - 1/21/47 Dog		**1982** 1/25/82 - 2/12/83 Dog	
1947 1/22/47 - 2/9/48 Pig	**1964** 2/13/64 - 2/1/65 Dragon	**1983** 2/13/83 - 2/1/84 Pig	**2000** 2/5/00 - 1/23/01 Dragon
1948 2/10/48 - 1/28/49 Rat	**1965** 2/2/65 - 1/20/66 Snake	**1984** 2/2/84 - 2/19/85 Rat	**2001** 1/24/01 - 2/11/02 Snake
1949 1/29/49 - 2/16/50 Ox	**1966** 1/21/66 - 2/8/67 Horse	**1985** 2/20/85 - 2/8/86 Ox	**2002** 2/12/02 - 1/31/03 Horse
1950 2/17/50 - 2/5/51 Tiger	**1967** 2/9/67 - 1/29/68 Ram	**1986** 2/9/86 - 1/28/87 Tiger	**2003** 2/1/03 - 1/21/04 Ram
1951 2/6/51 - 1/26/52 Rabbit	**1968** 1/30/68 - 2/16/69 Monkey	**1987** 1/29/87 - 2/16/88 Rabbit	**2004** 1/22/04 - 2/8/05 Monkey
	1969 2/17/69 - 2/5/70 Rooster	**1988** 2/17/88 - 2/5/89 Dragon	**2005** 2/9/05 - 1/28/06 Rooster
1952 1/27/52 - 2/13/53 Dragon	**1970** 2/6/70 - 1/26/71 Dog		**2006** 1/29/06 - 2/17/07 Dog
1953 2/14/53 - 2/2/54 Snake	**1971** 1/27/71 - 2/15/72 Pig	**1989** 2/6/89 - 1/26/90 Snake	**2007** 2/18/07 - 2/6/08 Pig
1954 2/3/54 - 1/23/55 Horse	**1972** 2/16/72 - 2/2/73 Rat	**1990** 1/27/90 - 2/14/91 Horse	**2008** 2/7/08 - 1/25/09 Rat
1955 1/24/55 - 2/11/56 Ram	**1973** 2/3/73 - 1/22/74 Ox	**1991** 2/15/91 - 2/3/92 Ram	**2009** 1/26//09 - 2/13/10 Ox
1956 2/12/56 - 1/30/57 Monkey	**1974** 1/23/74 - 2/10/75 Tiger	**1992** 2/4/92 - 1/22/93 Monkey	**2010** 2/14/10 - 2/2/11 Tiger
1957 1/31/57 - 2/17/58 Rooster	**1975** 2/11/75 - 1/30/76 Rabbit	**1993** 1/23/93 - 2/9/94 Rooster	**2011** 2/3/11 - 1/22/12 Rabbit
			2012 1/23/12 - 2/9/13 Dragon

Vera's Chinese Horoscope
September 28, 1940

Dragon people are the most eccentric in the Chinese Zodiac.

Soaring high into the serene heavens, they can be stubborn, passionate, excitable, honest, and brave, wear purple and walk barefoot in public fountains. They listen to their own drummer, thank you very much, while the rest of the world stands in amazement. People always admire their individuality and feisty personality.

Dragons are capable of doing great work for mankind and they inspire trust in almost everyone. The Dragon symbolizes life and growth and is said to bring the five blessings: harmony, virtue, riches, fulfillment and longevity. Everything these Dragons touch turns to gold. They hold top positions of responsibility in their careers and are revered for their peals of wisdom and dynamic leadership.

The Metal Dragon, you see, has always had the "right stuff" to make it big, ambition, unflagging enthusiasm, supreme confidence, intelligence and the quirky creativity necessary to make a beautiful life. Life is beautiful, no worries for the Metal Dragon, who is one of the few who experience the freedom of true security.

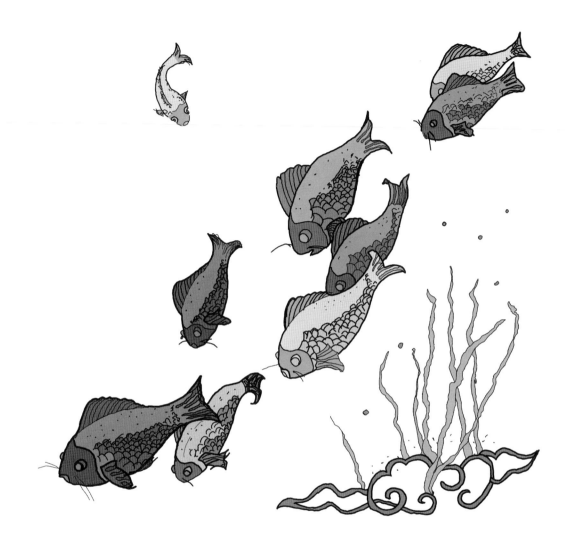

Golden Pond

The Little Fish in the Big Pond

Golden Pond
The Little Fish in the Big Pond

Would you rather be the big fish in the little pond or the little fish in the big golden pond? Like most of my ABC friends, I thought I would be happy being a big fish in the small community pond. However, I found that in small community ponds, there are pecking orders that limit a person's growth. Wanting to broaden my horizons, I gingerly tried the big pond. It was uncharted waters, with unexpected undercurrents, but there were also greater opportunities and rewards. The big pond's diverse people and varied outlooks were energizing. There, people take you at face value. There are no predetermined expectations based on your family's place in the community. Throughout the years, I've jumped in, and even if I came up short of my goals, just having made the attempt has helped me expand my sensitivity and support networks.

I attended Garfield High School from 1955 to 1958. During this time, I found out that sometimes losing brings forth new opportunities. In my senior year, I tried out for cheerleader and lost. Not wanting to sit on the sidelines in my senior year, I ran successfully for senior class secretary and became the features editor of the school paper. As it turned out, this stroke of fate gave me better grounding for my future career and for my later community involvement. Through these high school activities, I was able to establish unexpected bonds of friendships that changed my life forever.

In the 1950s, Garfield High School had a balanced ethnic and racial mix. Back then, African Americans were called Negroes, Asian Americans were called Orientals and European Americans were called Caucasians. The student body consisted of kids from the

wealthy gated community of Broadmoor as well the children of blue-collar workers. There was equal representation of the different groups, and an easy rapport between all of us in student government and sports. I have remained lifelong friends with many of my friends from this diverse crowd.

Broadmoor resident Tim Tucker and I were on a class committee together and became casual friends. I liked teasing him and calling him "little Timmy Tucker." Tim's childhood friend was Herbert "Budd" Gould III, who graduated from Queen Anne the same year as we did. Both went on to become stockbrokers. In the early 1970s, Tim and Budd decided to go into business together. They hired my husband Joey to do a small remodel of their first restaurant, the Red Fox, at the Crossroads Shopping Center in Bellevue. Tim went back to being a stockbroker. When we started investing seriously, he was our account executive until he retired. Budd went on to develop the multiple Anthony's Restaurants. Joey has designed them all. Through the 35 year association Joey and I have had with the Goulds, we have celebrated birthdays, second marriages, children's weddings, memorials, and holidays together in Budd's homes in Sun Valley, Hawaii and Whidbey Island. There have been many memorable moments.

In the late 1990s, Budd and Kathy invited us to their small wedding in Hawaii. Besides their blended family, there were only two other couples besides Tim and Melissa and Joey and myself. The wedding was held at sunset on the grounds of the Mauna Lani Resort at the historic Parker Ranch facing the ocean. We went to the open market and bought flowers and fresh fruit. I made a three-foot bridal bouquet out of orchid sprays held together with a paper plate with a fork stuck through the back, and I decorated the grounds with orchid-festooned Walmart tiki torches. Sharon Kramis, Anthony's longtime food consultant, cooked the wedding supper of kalbi ribs and huli huli chicken purchased at the Parker Ranch. The women all wore hats and flowing muu-muus that moved with the wind. Later, we did the same thing for Tim and Melissa Tucker's wedding.

Best friends from Garfield High School. Top right: Jan Sakamoto. Bottom left: Lorita Delma. Bottom right: Jan Kudo – Author's photo.

Gould wedding in Kona, Hawaii
– Author's photo.

We have also shared some frightening experiences. Once, we never thought we would make it coming back from Sun Valley, Idaho. After driving all day, we encountered a heavy snowstorm approaching Snoqualmie Pass on Interstate-90 late at night. The pounding snow was coming right at us, and none of us could see a thing. Joey was driving white-knuckled and Budd was talking nervously non-stop. Kathy Gould and I were in the back seat being very quiet. I closed my eyes and prayed. All of a sudden, there was a stunned silence because the snow magically stopped. Although we couldn't see the approach, we had just entered the

*Dolores Sibonga and Fred Pausell
at Vera's 40th birthday
– Author's photo.*

snow shed near the summit. It looked like we had entered a dream world. Once we passed the tunnel, the snow was much more gentle and we made it home to safety.

On another trip, we got lost on our way to the Pasadena Rose Bowl. All of a sudden, Budd started speeding and honking loudly at another car, urging them to pull over, while Larry Kramis was pretending to moon them. At the time, there were many stories of road rage on the L.A. freeways and I was sure we would be shot. It turned out it to be Tim Tucker in the other car. I exclaimed to Budd, "How could you have known it was Tim, going 65 miles a hour down the L.A. freeway when you're both in rental cars?" Budd simply replied: "I'd know that ugly face anywhere."

Through our long-term professional relationship with the Goulds, we have been able, with their patronage, to support a community college scholarship endowment fund and make a significant contribution to the Wing Luke Asian Museum's capital campaign to remodel the East Kong Yick Building into its new home.

Another friend was Fred Paulsell, a fellow Garfield High school class officer who was a couple years ahead of me. Fred wrote in my school album to "aim high." That was a pretty serious message, since most of my classmates wrote things like "Have a great summer" or "Kiss the boys for me." In 1967, nine years after we graduated from Garfield, we found ourselves – with our respective families – living just four houses away from one another in the Mt. Baker neighborhood overlooking Lake Washington where the Seafair Hydroplane Races are held. We had moved to Mt. Baker during the Boeing Company slump when many white families fled to the suburbs. Many of the fine homes in the area had been boarded up, the neighborhood was in transition because of racial tension, and the banks would not make conventional loans there. There were many boarded-up homes in the neighborhood that had been repossessed by the Department of Housing and Urban Devel-

3/24 Lakewood Ave.
MT. BAKER PK. B-69. L-18.

Mt. Baker house as it looked in the 1930s
– Assessor's photo, WA State Archives,
Puget Sound Branch.

opment (HUD). Some folks were even able to get dilapidated houses in the neighborhood on the condition that they provide the sweat equity to bring the home up to code.

Fred was managing director of a brokerage firm and an early investor in Costco and Ballard Computers. He and Marsha Paulsell could have afforded to live anywhere. Our move to Mt. Baker was pure serendipity. After we moved Ah Ma to another nursing home more to her liking – this one between Rainer Avenue and Empire Way (now Martin Luther King Jr. Way) – we put our Beacon Hill house on the market for $15,000 so we could find a lot to build our own home.

We had budgeted $25,000 for a new home, which Joey would design. Our plan was to spend $2,000 on a lot near a good school, since our oldest was starting first grade. We made several unsuccessful offers on lots by Seward Park and by the former dump between Lake Washington Blvd and Genesee. We wanted to live in these areas so our children could attend Graham Hill Elementary School or Hawthorne Elementary School.

Out of curiosity, I went to an open house in the Mt. Baker neighborhood near a lot we had hoped to purchase. The house was vacant, badly neglected and had been on the market for over two years. It was selling for $45,000, way beyond our means. But it had a wonderful water view and the scale of the floor plan gave me a sense of comfort, which I now attribute to the house's good feng shui. I didn't know a thing about feng shui at the time. Years later I bought several books on the subject when it became popular to design projects based on feng shui principles. As it turned out, our house had good feng shui. It was located in front of Lake Washington, water representing good chi, bringing good fortune to its residents. Across the street from the front of the house was a small hill, providing symbolic support for the family through difficult times. And the house had a good yin-yang balance, represented by good sunlight, shade, wind and moisture along Lake Washington Boulevard.

We decided to make a $30,000 offer on the house – $15,000 less than the asking price, but still $5,000 over the amount we had budgeted. We never dreamed that the offer would even be seriously considered. To make things even harder, we added a contingency that we would have four months to renovate before taking possession. Several weeks later, to our surprise, the sellers accepted our offer. I'm guessing that it was probably the only offer they had received.

Growing up in the Central Area, I remembered taking the Number 10 Mt. Baker bus and passing the large fine homes to go swimming at the Mt. Baker Beach, never dreaming that I could ever live there. Now, years later, I was getting ready to move into the neighborhood.

After feeling like we had won the lottery, buyer's remorse set in. The neighborhood school, John Muir Elementary, was not the school I wanted our children to attend. Because the neighborhood was in transition, Mt. Baker had been "redlined," meaning that banks were reluctant to approve loans in the area. Therefore, the bank required us to put down $10,000 on our $30,000 home, leaving us with nothing in our savings account. The monthly mortgage payments were twice as much as our Beacon Hill house. Joey had just opened his own architectural firm the year before when he was asked to design the 13 Coins Restaurant on Boren Avenue. But there were no new major projects on the boards. What had we gotten ourselves into?

I also worried how the longtime Mt. Baker neighbors would receive us. It's one thing to

Jeannie and Vera at the Okimoto's Mt. Baker home – Author's photo.

explore the big pond, but moving your entire nest to unfamiliar territory is another matter.

Before moving in, I loaded up my beat-up old station wagon with my sisters Helen and Mari and Mari's five children – all under 10 – and my three children – all under 5 – and drove to the new house. Our next door neighbor, Miss Smith, an unmarried woman who looked to be in her 60s, stared at us from the adjacent driveway, speechless. Miss Smith had been born in her house. I reacted to her silence by speaking in rapid Chinese to Mari, telling her that I was going to have trouble with "that one." Miss Smith's first impression of us must have been that we were one of those huge immigrant families not yet conversant in English.

The painting and remodel of the kitchen turned out to be a nightmare. Joey was able to get custom-made teak kitchen cabinets at cost from the woodworking company that did the 13 Coins cabinetry. After buying bargain appliances at the Sears Outlet Store, we thought it would be simple and inexpensive to retrofit the kitchen. We didn't realize how difficult it would be to tear down the plaster and chicken wire walls or how antiquated the electrical system was in homes built at the turn of the century.

There were scary moments working late at night in a large unfamiliar vacant house. I felt uneasy going in the windowless basement storage area. The large freezer left there reminded me of a coffin. I put a large mirror in the space and somehow the area seemed less gloomy. Late one night we were scared when we uncovered a hidden door in one of the kitchen walls, which just turned out to be another door to the front hall.

In 1967, two weeks before Christmas, we moved into our new home. Our kitchen was still incomplete. A moving van moved out the large freezer and the furnishings left in the house. Brother-in-law Kai and Joey's buddy Tom Ko rented a U-Haul truck and helped us move our own things into the house. I remember the moment of panic when the truck slowly started to roll as they were unloading because the parking brakes were not set tightly.

*Joel and Josh Schroeter
– Author's photo.*

To make our new home feel more inviting, I placed a gold tabletop Christmas tree in the entrance hall. Exhausted, we fell asleep together among the unpacked boxes in the living room. The Christmas tree is still part of our annual Christmas decorations, as are three golden stockings we received the day after we moved in.

I've learned that first impressions can be deceiving. It turned out that Miss Smith was the first of our immediate neighbors who came calling to welcome us the morning after we moved in. Miss Smith gave our children the three candy-filled golden stockings that we still

use every Christmas. She also brought flowers from Crissey's Florist, considered, at that time, the primo flower shop. I found out that she stuttered and that was the reason she didn't speak to us when we were in the driveway.

The Bucks, next door to Miss Smith, came to visit us shortly afterwards, bringing a plate of holiday cookies. Five-year-old Josh Schroeter, next door to us, rang the door and asked if our son Joel could come out to play. As he came into the entrance and saw the gold Christmas tree, he declared: "I knew you would be Christians!" Josh and Joel remain friends today.

Throughout the holiday season, we were embraced by many residents. Neighbors like Jack and Shirley Sullivan would invite new residents like us to potlucks before a community club event. Artis and Pete Palmer, who lived down our street, invited everyone on the block over for hot chocolate and dessert when it snowed. Other Lakewood Street neighbors like Josh's mother, Dorothy Schroeter, who later became Mayor Charles Royer's executive administrator, and Jeanne Kirkman, whose husband worked in Fred's brokerage firm, became everyday friends.

Our next door neighbor looked after our children in the same way that Auntie Florence looked after me when I was living in Canton Alley. Joel spent most of his days next door playing with Josh, until the Schroeters left to live in Israel a few years later. Just before leaving, Josh spent the night with us on Christmas Eve and opened presents along with the family. The boys were too young to write letters, so they corresponded through drawings. Josh called Joel from the airport upon returning to Seattle two years later. Dorothy told me that call was the deciding factor for them to move back to Mt. Baker. The boys grew up together. We went to Josh's Bar Mitzvah. He came for celebration of Chinese New Year. After college Joel and Josh both worked in New York and both moved back to Seattle after they married. Josh married a neighborhood classmate and lives in Mt. Baker with his own family. Joel married Long Island-born attorney Audrey Hwang; they now live in Seattle's Montlake neighborhood. Joel and Audrey recently went to Josh and Lisa's daughter's Bat Mitzvah.

Our new neighbors in Mt. Baker were young attorneys, stockbrokers, public administrators, shop owners, former Peace Corps workers and future politicians united in the goal of coming together as a community to turn things around. Motivated by the need to protect our children and our investment in the big pond, I joined the Mt. Baker Community Club's efforts to improve the neighborhood's schools, housing and public safety.

The most immediate issue was dealing with sending our children to John Muir Elementary. The neighborhood school was in turmoil partly because the mostly-minority school had 900 students in a building only meant for 600 students. The halls were lined up with children waiting to be disciplined by the school principal, who seemed overwhelmed. My first grade daughter JaDeane was afraid to go to the bathroom during school and begged to go to a private or Catholic school. One of the hardest things is for a parent is to send a child to an unsafe school and know that you can't afford to do anything else. I told JaDeane that while she shouldn't be intimidated, she was also smart enough to walk away from trouble. Her dad became her hero when he walked into her classroom and told the bathroom bully to leave JaDeane alone and then walked out without waiting for her response or without saying a word to the teacher. Jay did fine after that show of support and has now become the street-smart kid in our family.

The neighborhood did not give up on the school, although that seemed to be the case for the overwhelmed, long-time school principal. Marsha and Jeanne also sent their children to John Muir, as did many Garfield High classmates. Two African American community

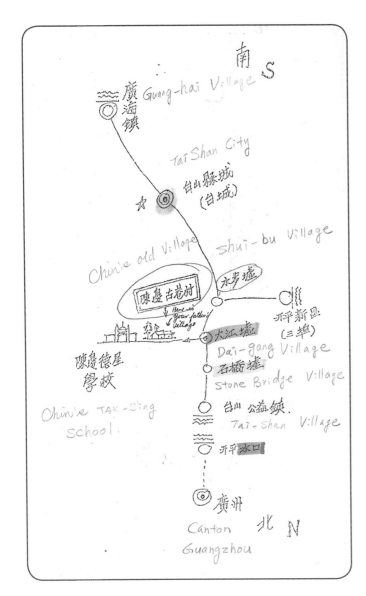

Alice Chan's sketch showing the location of Ah Ba's village.

activists, John Little and his brother Ernie, helped organize the diverse parents and joined others in patrolling the hallways and bathrooms, tutoring kids and lobbying the Seattle School Board for improvements to the school. Ernie came to School Board meetings in a large Afro, dark sunglasses, dashiki shirts, wearing tons of heavy gold. No group was more committed or felt ownership of the school more than the African American parents.

The School Board moved the younger students to the school portable facility on Mt. Baker Ridge. Neighbors Charles Huey, Jeanne Okimoto and Dexter and Virginia Washburn were instrumental in securing a new principal who was sensitive and greatly interested in the success of the students. Earl Sedlik got City funding to organize the parents to clean up and convert a neglected street into a hillside park with steps, making it safer for the students to walk to school.

One neighbor, Marilyn Coo, organized the first Martin Luther King, Jr. Day celebration for the Mt. Baker Community Club. As a member of Mt. Zion Baptist Church, she was able to secure the Total Experience Choir to perform at the celebration. It was one of the most inclusive and successful events during those early days of community action. She and Gary Edwards later founded the Mt. Baker Community Club's Martin Luther King, Jr. Scholarship Program during my watch as Club President.

The Parent-Teacher Association was one of the most active in the School District. As more neighbors got involved in the school, more neighbors sent their children to the public schools. John Muir Elementary had one of the most balanced student populations and most successful academic records in Seattle before the mandatory-busing program. The goals of mandatory-busing were to achieve an ethnically balanced school population and quality academic achievement through the City. Since the Mt. Baker neighborhood had worked hard to achieve those goals already, the Community Club was divided as to whether to support this referendum. In the end, the neighborhood stayed true to its values of equality and supported the busing program.

I believe that, in retrospect, the goals of mandatory busing were not achieved. Students bused in to a school from outside the community where they live tend to stick together in the classrooms and the lunchroom. It is difficult to participate in activities and develop new friendships when you're trying to follow strict bus schedules and you aren't really part of the neighborhood. Many of the John Muir parents enrolled their children in private schools or found ways to keep them in the neighborhood schools.

Another neighbor on our block, Artis Palmer, started a support group for "at risk" students. She asked my next door neighbor Dorothy Schroeter to tutor African American students, many of whom were members of the militant Black Panther Party. Artis asked me to tutor immigrant students from Hong Kong.

At that time, homes on our block were robbed regularly. Many of the high school students, including Dorothy's sons, were harassed and robbed while they were walking to school. Once, while Dorothy's family was sleeping upstairs, someone broke into the house and stole an heirloom rug. She mentioned this to the students she was tutoring. The next day, the rug was returned to our driveway, wrapped in a New York City newspaper.

The female Chinese students I tutored became part of our extended family. Unable to afford college, many of them had no greater aspirations than to wait on tables before settling down. I encouraged them to go to community college since it was accessible and affordable. Emily, one of the students, came to live with us, making it possible for me to go back to University of Washington full-time. Alice Chan came from the same village as Ah Ba, knew where my father's house was in China and drew a map so that I might one day go back to visit. Alice married an ABC engineer; and their children made it into Ivy League colleges. Another student, Linda, married Auntie Florence's younger son. Fannie became a career woman.

There were times when I worried about the future of my male charges in high school. Some got suspended for knife fights with other students. One got in trouble later for fighting with a security guard. One student "borrowed" my guitar without returning it. Their stories of the deaths and poverty they had witnessed before immigrating to America made me worry if reactive violence may have become part of their survival instinct. Although I wasn't sure I could help, they attended the weekly tutoring sessions at our house without fail and were open to my mothering. Some of the boys became soccer coaches for the Mt. Baker teams. A few years later, one of the former soccer coaches came for assistance with a manslaughter warrant hanging over him. As to why he deserved a second chance, he would respond: "But Mrs. Ing, I didn't run away."

Somehow, all of these kids survived their troubled youth. Today they are fathers, businessmen and leaders in the Chinese community. In the 1980s, they came to my husband's rescue when Chinatown leaders held a public meeting at the Chong Wa Benevolent Association and attempted to discredit the newly-formed International Special Review District Board. The Board had proposed zoning changes that would have moved storefront family associations up to the second floors of buildings. Joey, Ray Chinn, Glenn Chinn, and the branch manager of SeaFirst Bank were sent to represent the Review Board. The Chong Wa hall was abuzz with the clamor of angry people. The banker seemed to be getting the brunt of the audience's rage. I was afraid that it was going to be a long unpleasant evening. Then I saw several of my former students waving at me. I pointed to Joey and gestured that he was my husband. Once they realized the situation, they walked out of the meeting as a group as a sign of support for him and me. The negative energy of the room was defused. It turned out to be a good meeting and many of those attending have since served on the Review Board.

When I ran for office in 1984, many of my former students were among the first to write a check and put out a campaign sign in their storefronts. I would have never taken the time to play a part in their lives had it not been for the encouragement and support of the Mt. Baker community.

Dexter and Virginia Washburn bought the next door house from the Schroeters after they moved to Israel. My youngest son Jeff and their youngest son Michael became play-mates. Now it was Jeff who spent most of his time next door, often staying for dinner. Unlike our family, where someone would be grabbing food off the table before running off to some meeting or activity, the Washburns were the kind of people who sat down together for dinner without interruptions from the phone. Jeff is the only one in the family who doesn't gobble down his food. Mike was one year younger than Jeff, but often served as his protector. Once I was in the kitchen watching them play outside on the sidewalk and heard an older neighbor ask Jeff what he was – Chinese or Japanese. Before I could confront her, Michael responded simply: "He's Jeff."

Being active in the community can also create opportunities to discover soul mates. When one of the students I was tutoring was in danger of being expelled from Franklin High School, someone suggested that I contact respected Asian community activist Dr. Joe Okimoto to help work things out. "Dr. Joe" gave up a promising career as a surgeon to become one of the community's leading psychiatrists. Dr. Joe, Don Kazama and Min Masuda helped establish the Asian Counseling and Referral Service (ACRS) in 1973, a time when there was very little understanding of or support for mental health services in the Asian Pacific American community.

ACRS was first housed at Blaine Memorial Methodist Church before it moved to the International District. It provided counseling and job training to newly arriving immigrants from Southeast Asia. In 2008, ACRS opened up a brand new $22 million facility in Southeast Seattle and has expanded its services to a much broader and diverse Asian American community. My husband Joey brings his Blaine Memorial Methodist Church men's group there for senior lunches. I look forward to taking dance lessons there someday, another senior activity. Another full circle.

Both Dr. Joe and my friend Jeanne Kirkman got divorced because their respective spouses did not share the same kind of commitment that they had to community service. Don Kazama felt Joe and Jeanne were soul mates and introduced the two to one another. They fell in love, and were married in Jeanne's Mt. Baker home in the presence of family and a couple of friends. It was the coolest wedding I have ever participated in. Jeanne wore a blue-and-white checkered gown. I was dressed in a patchwork 1970s dress, with a barrette pulling back my long hair. I opened the ceremony by singing John Denver's, "Today, while the blossoms still cling to the vine ..." Pastor Morgan, another neighbor friend, read from Kahlil Gibran's "The Prophet," while dressed in a white Filipino shirt. Joe closed the ceremony by singing the classic love song "Jean" from "The Prime of Miss Jean Brodie." The wedding supper for 12 was in a private dining room at the Olympic Hotel, with a menu of Northwest salmon and spinach salad; at the time, we wanted to honor the boycott of lettuce and grapes to support Cesar Chavez's efforts to establish the United Farm Workers Union. Jeanne became a therapist and an award-winning author of children's books. Dr. Joe Okimoto still carries on his practice. They have been married for over 35 years.

Before we moved into the neighborhood, the Mt. Baker Community Club was strictly a social club, and activities centered on monthly formal dances. The historic club pictures are of the men of the neighborhood dressed up in top hats and morning coats on New Year's Day, getting ready to go calling on residents, and of costume parties where some of the participants are made up in black face or have their eyes pulled taut with tape to mimic the look of an "Oriental." While there was a covenant that all property owners within the neighborhood boundaries automatically become members of the Community Club, there were no people of color in any of the historic pictures.

Jack Sullivan, Junius Rochester, Fred Paulsell, Glover Barnes, Earl Sedlik and other Community Club presidents of the 1970s changed the focus to neighborhood revitalization and cohesiveness among the increasingly diverse residents in the neighborhood. The neighborhood was fortunate to have a run of Community Club presidents who provided the leadership needed to spark neighborhood-wide participation.

Being Mt. Baker Community Club president is a demanding position. Former Mayor Norm Rice said that serving as Community Club president was harder than being Mayor. Many years later, when I held that position, I discovered hate mail from the 1960s in the Club archives from older neighbors complaining about how the Club was run and how the neighborhood was being ruined because of too many ethnic minorities were moving into the area. When Joey and I first moved to Mt. Baker, I had thought that when the Sullivans, the Burns and the Palmers had invited us to potlucks before a Community Club event, they were just kindly "white folks" being polite to us. Now I knew, in retrospect, that these seemingly courteous gestures were, in fact, very courageous acts.

To instill community pride in the early days as we began to rehabilitate the neighborhood, Janice Rochester organized a Mt. Baker district home tour. Fred and Marsha Paulsell extensively remodeled their fine home to its former grandeur in time for our first tour. The Paulsells refurbished a Tiffany glass ceiling hidden above the plasterboard ceiling in their entry hall and had custom-made furniture, carpets and flooring made for the tour.

Our house was also featured in the first home tour. When I agreed for us to be part of the event, I was way too busy completing my first quarter back at the college. Besides taking final exams, I was also opening an art gallery on the street level of Joey's office in time for holiday sales. Somehow everything fell neatly into place and our house was the one selected to be featured in Dorothy Byrant Braizer's column in *The Seattle Times*. The column was about being able to multi-task and our homemade Christmas tree decorations, made with sugar cones and pink tissue paper.

The 1970s era of community development block grants gave a big boost to the renewal of Mt. Baker. I worked with Community Club members Bruce Hurst and Vivianne Strickler to help lobby the Seattle City Council so that Mt. Baker would be selected as one of the eight neighborhoods eligible for Neighborhood Housing Rehabilitation Funds. Upon completion of my degree in urban planning from the University of Washington in 1974, the Seattle Housing Authority hired me as the Mt. Baker Neighborhood Housing Rehabilitation community organizer.

These neighborhood organizing efforts bonded us. Ike Banks, who served on the Neighborhood Housing Rehabilitation Board, encouraged Joey to apply for the renovation design contract for the Seattle Urban League headquarters on 14th Avenue and Yesler Way. The building was across the street from the original location of the Mutual Fish Company, run by several generations of the Yoshimura family, with connections to the ABC community. Al Mar's Grocery was on the street level. The upstairs apartments were the first homes of returning World War II veterans Warren Chan, Art Chin and Ben Woo and their new brides.

I still recall how happy and surprised we were when Ike called the office to tell us that we had been awarded the contract. Joey and I scooped up our preschool son Jeff and we all danced around. It was the largest fee we had ever been awarded. At that time, our fees ranged around $5,000. The Urban League fee was $42,000, and, even after engineering and other sub-consultant feels, we managed to bank nearly $25,000. That nest egg gave us the needed boost to buy our own building.

The Urban League design project also forged many special friendships. Besides Ike, Seattle's Urban League Director Jerome Page, Board Member Constance Acholono, and student intern Norm Rice became part of our Mt. Baker family.

Later, Norm enjoyed a very successful political career, first serving on the Seattle City Council from 1987 to 1998, then as a very popular two-term Seattle Mayor from 1990 to 1997. We were among the small group of friends at Norm's wedding to Constance at April Eng's house in Madison Park. During Norm's first run for the Seattle City Council, we donated our office space in the International District for his campaign. Joey and I celebrated birthdays, anniversaries and holidays together in the 1970s and '80s with the Rices and the Okimotos. We would usually cap off the evening at our house by getting out the guitars and singing folk songs.

One year, our college-aged daughter's Christmas Eve flight from the East Coast was diverted to Portland because of heavy fog. After sorting out all the options, we decided the best solution was for our sons to drive down to pick her up. Joel was designated the driver, and Jeff's job was to keep him awake. I was so worried that there might be an accident. The Rices and KOMO-TV Reporter Connie Thompson and her husband Don stayed with us, singing Christmas carols until our three children made the six-hour round-trip journey home safely.

It was exciting being in the big pond, but things were not very constant. Fred Paulsell, Jack Sullivan, Bruce Hurst, Dorothy Schroeter and other neighbors have passed away. The Rices, Palmers, Stricklers and Sally Hurst remain in Mt. Baker, but we rarely see them. While they remain dear friends, Mt. Baker neighbors like the Washburns and Okimotos are enjoying their just rewards and have moved to fancy condos downtown or to island homes.

Today, I walk through the beautifully-staged open houses on our block and reflect on how much the neighborhood has improved since the early days. This has happened without gentrification. It is still a diverse community working together. At times, Joey and I have considered selling our house and building an apartment above our little office building downtown, but we have lived in our home for 40 years and it's hard to let go of good memories.

Instead, we decided to remodel our kitchen once again. We refinished our teak office conference table top to use as the kitchen island. We also refinished the teak cabinets from the 1967 remodel. They look as good as new. Joey was able to fit the 1967 teak cabinets into the new space perfectly, just like putting a puzzle together. That retrofit is symbolic of the jigsaw puzzle of our life here.

Perhaps it was good feng shui after all. The Chinese believe successes and failure in life are often linked to the home, and that good feng shui positioning in the family home creates harmonious relationships, good health, prosperity and honor. I'm not sure I have been able to accomplish everything I've wanted to do in life, but I certainly can't complain.

Living in a big pond neighborhood like Mt. Baker has enriched our lives immensely. Maintaining connections to the community pond has made it possible to find our way back to the lifelong support and friendships of family and ABC friends. It is the best of both worlds.

Feng Shui Principles

Feng Shui literally means Wind and Water. It is the ancient Chinese art of positioning the home and work-place for positive interaction with the forces of nature to promote health, relationships, and career/self actualization. The principles determine:

1. A lucky building site.
2. The best way to position a building on a lot.
3. Floor plan and furniture arrangements.

The Chinese believe that positive Feng Shui placements can promote and result in harmonious family relationships, love, health, wealth, and honor. As in any art, becoming an expert takes study and practical experience. Like interior design, there are no absolute rules. My friends all know I am constantly changing my furniture placements. This can be attributed to being a frustrated decorator, Feng Shui superstition, or just wanting to make our guests comfortable and being able to circulate/converse easily whether it is an intimate party or reception for 100.

The Feng Shui approach is to find the arrangement that makes the users comfortable in their surroundings or to change their luck. There are no easy fixes. Monitor the changes for small transformations of luck and behavior. For example, for many years, our bed was positioned in front of the door, a Feng Shui no-no. When I moved the bed against the wall out of line of the door, but still facing the entrance, our martial relationship seemed to improve. Our friend's son was gravely ill and I saw that the young couple's bed was facing a mirrored closet wall and had a mirrored headboard. I suggested removing all the mirrors and his health improved. I'm not sure if it was only Feng Shui that changed things for the better, but if you see something you can change, it doesn't hurt to try.

There are many Feng Shui books that suggest positive positioning.

Feng Shui "cures" of unlucky immovable placements includes using vegetation, lucky symbols, plants, mirrors, lighting, screen/room dividers, colors, ceiling fans, and fish tanks to promote or deflect ch'i or energy for the benefit of the users. Creating positive Feng Shui ch'i in a room enhances individual emotional ch'i. Allow time for benign ch'i currents to slowly attract harmony and balance into your life. Have fun!

If nothing else, it will motivate you to maintain your home because, according to Feng Shui, the condition of your home mirrors your own health and relationships.

Golden Era

International District Community Action

Golden Era

International District Community Action

*T*he 1970s marked a golden period of community action. Neighborhoods like the International District went through a period of rebirth. It was great to witness the young college-aged students stepping forward – along with community leaders like Bob Santos and business leaders like Tomio Moriguchi – to fight for better housing, social services, arts and culture, street improvements and restoration of historic buildings.

It was exciting to be a part of that golden period, but I never did feel comfortable waving protest signs or leading the pack. Often I felt like the Peter Sellers' character in the movie "Being There," a serendipitous supporter or observer.

Nonetheless, my ABC upbringing, education in urban planning and love for the International District – shaped by my time growing up in Canton Alley and my parents' Chinatown restaurant – did prompt me to become involved. Even in the midst of conflicts between different factions in the community – especially when there were arguments between the activists and some of those who were more traditional in their thinking – I tried to understand the other side and consider compromises that would help us get to our goals.

I remember the 1960s as a troubled and violent era. John Kennedy, Martin Luther King Jr. and Robert Kennedy were assassinated. The unpopularity of the Vietnam War triggered local and national protests. The 1965 riot in the African American neighborhood of Watts, Los Angeles brought racial tensions to the fore. This spilled over into cities across the country, including Seattle where African Americans, many of whom lived in the Central Area, took to the streets. Longtime Chinese residents in the Central Area became fearful for their safety and

sold their homes for very little. We sold my mother's houses for one-third of their value after her tenants were hassled repeatedly and even hit when they dared walk down the street.

During this period of heightened awareness about the problems of poverty and discrimination and the problems in the intercity, the U.S. Congress passed the 1965 Voting Rights Act and the 1968 federal Fair Housing Act. Addressing the unfairness of immigration laws, the Congress also passed the Immigration and Nationality Act of 1965, which relaxed the restrictive quotas on immigration from Asia.

In 1974, Congress established the Community Development Block Grant Program, with the goal of eliminating poverty and "urban blight." Grant funds were given directly to the cities to use for neighborhood rehabilitation, housing and social services. I was the Seattle Housing Authority's first Community Development Block Grant Manager.

This set the stage for leaders in the International District like Bob Santos, director of Inter*Im (International District Improvement Association), to lobby government officials to provide funding to support community projects. Working alongside "Uncle Bob" – and sometimes acting as loud voices of protest – were student activists like Alan Sugiyama, Doug Chin and Frankie Irigon, who had been involved in pushing for affirmative action and promoting Asian American identity and unity on college campuses.

Throughout the 1970s, Bob and the International District activists organized community demonstrations and mobilized residents, owners of small restaurants and shops, and young Asian American professionals to speak out about the needs of the I.D. They lobbied the City and federal officials and were able to secure the funding to develop hundreds of units of low-income housing for seniors and low-income residents and establish bilingual social service agencies like the Asian Counseling and Referral Service and the International District Community Health Clinic, now the International Community Health Services.

John Woo's mural on the facade of the Bush Hotel – Ed Echtle photo.

An important instrument for community preservation and development has been the Seattle Chinatown-International District Preservation and Development Authority (SCIDPDA). The agency, chartered by the City in 1975, receives funding to develop housing, restore historic buildings and develop new projects that add economic and cultural vitality to the neighborhood.

Two organizations – Inter*Im, led by Bob Santos, and the Chong Wa Benevolent Association, led by Ruby Chow and her allies – vied for control when the SCIDPDA was being established. In the end, the control tilted toward Inter*Im, but in a concession to Chong Wa, the Mayor insisted on addition of the word "Chinatown" to the name of the organization. Through the years, most of the individuals who have served on Inter*Im's board have also served on the SCIDPDA board as well.

The first major SCIDPDA project was the development of a new community center for the International District. Shigeko Uno, working as property manager for Rainier Heat

and Power, which owned the hotel, brokered the sale of the historic Bush Hotel on Jackson Street to the SCIDPDA in 1978. Shigeko was also the one who convinced Tomio Moriguchi to purchase another Rainier Heat and Power property to develop his family's Uwajimaya supermarket.

The "Bush-Asia Center" project was the first major mixed-use development in the International District in the 1970s. With financial support from the City, the Bush Hotel was remodeled into low-income and transient housing on the upper floors, and office space for social service agencies and small shops on the lower levels.

At the same time that Bob Santos and other Asian American activists were fighting for the International District, other activists of color were working in their communities as well, leaders such as Larry Gossett, who was director of the Central Area Motivation Program; Bernie Whitebear, who established the United Indians of All Tribes Foundation and the Daybreak Star Center in Discovery Park; and Roberto Maestas, director of El Centro de la Raza on Beacon Hill. These leaders were close allies and supported one another on policy and funding issues.

During the golden era of the 1970s and early 1980s, I served on the board of Inter*Im and the SCIDPDA and many Asian American social service agencies, but my passion remained in the arts. I believe that community arts are a powerful way to tell our stories and bring us all together. The Wing Luke Asian Museum and Northwest Asian American Theatre became mainstays of the community. Public art was installed throughout the neighborhood. Asian American artists began to come into their own and achieve recognition not only within the community, but also in the larger society.

SCIDPDA projects required that one percent of all construction funding be set aside for art. The Tsutakawa family – famed artist and sculptor George Tsutakawa, his wife Ayame, daughter Mayumi and son Gerard – were key players in the I.D. public art projects. Mayumi Tsutakawa, longtime arts administrator, was art competition coordinator for street banners and for a mural project on the south façade of the Bush Hotel. Ben Woo's son, John, was given the commission to create the mural, which depicts a large dragon interwoven with images of Asian American labor history.

I asked George Tsutakawa, who by that time was recognized as one of Japan's living treasures, if he could do a piece of art for the I.D for the small sum of $5,000, money budgeted for art from a streetscaping project. George agreed to do it, creating an incredible twelve-foot tall, four-sided bronze sculpture to symbolize the harmony, unity and the growth of the community at that time. It is on the southeast corner of Maynard Avenue and South Jackson Street.

Two new public parks provided badly needed open space for residents. Next to the Bush Hotel is Hing Hay Park, built in the 1970s, featuring a traditional Chinese pavilion and serving as the staging area for the annual Chinatown-International District Summer Festival. John Woo's mural is clearly visible from Hing Hay Park.

The International Children's Park on South Lane Street is the other major park in the

International Children's Park dragon by Gerard Tsutukawa
— Ed Echtle photos.

I.D. When Joey's architectural firm was awarded the design for the International Children's Park, we hired Gerard Tsutakawa to design a climbing dragon sculpture as the centerpiece. I asked Gerry to create something that might serve as an iconic image for the I.D., much like the Ming Dynasty camels in front of the Seattle Asian Art Museum in Volunteer Park. Gerry's climbing dragon is still a must-see image for visitors to the I.D. It was Gerry's first major commission. Gerry has since gone on to become one of the most respected sculptors in the Pacific Northwest, following in the footsteps of his late father.

The International Children's Park design incorporates influences from the three major pioneer Asian American groups: the Chinese, Japanese and Filipinos. The Chinese dragon in the sand and grass areas are designed in the yin and yang pattern. The Japanese pioneers are represented by the neon parasol shelter, and the Filipino community is represented by the swing bridge and climbing rock "hill." It was a project of great pride to Joey and myself, and I know Joey and landscape consultant Tom Berger put in many more hours than we charged for.

One of my continuing passions has been the Wing Luke Asian Museum. The Museum was named in honor of Wing Luke, the first Asian American elected official in the Pacific Northwest, a strong civil rights advocate who became our very first role model in the political arena. Ben Woo, Ark Chin, Warren Chan and Faith Enyeart helped launch the Wing Luke Memorial Museum in 1967 in a 1,500 square foot storefront on Eighth Avenue, a space donated by Chin Han's relatives. Exhibits featured heirloom clothing and artifacts from families of the Chinatown pioneers.

The Museum was open whenever board members agreed to volunteer. The annual budget depended on whatever the annual art auction brought in.

In the early years, the auction was a small event. It would start at the Chong Wa Benevolent Association, then move over to the Museum. Ruby Chow would donate the chow mein, fried rice, chicken wings and alcohol. Ben Woo would pour free drinks in an effort to spur the bidding along. Diane Sugimura, who would later become director of planning and development for the City of Seattle, Nobie Chan, longtime trustee of the Seattle Community College District, and I would bid against each other for art by notable Asian artists like Ron Ho, George Tsutakawa, Fay Chong, Frank Fujii, Joshel Namkung and Andrew Chinn. The winning bid was often under $500. Joey and I got many fine art pieces in those days for under $100. Rita Elway (now Rita Brogan) would start the bidding at $10 without even seeing what the item was; she usually won while everyone else was in line for food.

The Museum began to expand its vision after the election of Glenn Chinn as President of the Board in the early 1970s. Glenn was committed to moving to larger quarters and expanding the Museum's focus. Knowing of my interest in community history and art, Glenn asked me to take on a bigger role. I had my first encounter with China politics when I served as the Museum's representative and coordinator of a Chinese week at the 1974 Spokane World's Fair. President Richard Nixon had just visited the People's Republic of China as the first step toward normalizing relations between the U.S. and China. In that era, all of the Chinese American entertainers in the U.S. had ties to Taiwan. The Canadian Chinese wanted me to present mainland Chinese entertainment. Chinese Americans threaten to walk out if I permitted that. I played my ABC – or ignorant *"jook sing"* card – and told both sides I was too dumb to deal with Asia politics, and would just schedule their acts on different days. It was the truth, and everything worked out.

Glenn also asked me be the auctioneer at the annual auction. Wearing Ah Ma's antique gown, 4-inch high heels and false eyelashes, I helped bring in a record $8,000. I suffered dearly the morning after the auction from wearing those darn pointed heels all night, but the windfall allowed us to hire Peg Marshall, a weaver, as the Museum's first paid part-time

left to right: Vera Ing, Ron Ho, Patti Warashina, Lucy Liu, Johsel Namkung, Nori Okamura, Midori Kono Thiel, Ayame Tsutakawa.

Wing Luke Asian Museum, "Made in America" Art Show Program, 1980 – Wing Luke Asian Museum archives.

director. Peg was Caucasian, but to her credit, she agreed with our vision to expand the Museum beyond the display of traditional Chinese heirlooms and bring in Northwest Asian American history and art.

Ayame Tsutakawa and Glenn Chinn initiated the Museum's first Asian American exhibits, featuring the works of renowned artists like George Tsutakawa and colleagues such as Fay Chong and Andrew Chinn. The following year I was able to expand on these earlier efforts with the help of *International Examiner* editor Ron Chew, writer Gary Iwamoto, and artist Jeff Hanada who assisted in the application for a grant from the Seattle Arts Commission, and with publicity. The 1980 exhibit, "Made in America," won high praise from the art critics at *The Seattle Times* and *Seattle Post-Intelligencer* and resulted in citywide recognition that Asian American artists have played and continue to play a vital role in the Northwest art scene. The participants included Frank Fujii, Ron Ho, Mits Katayama, Val Laigo, Lucy Liu, John Matsudaira, Josel Namkung, Frank Okada, Nori Okamura, Mark Sato, Roger Shimomura, Midori Kono Thiel, George Tsutakawa, Gerard Tsutakawa and Patti Warashina. "Made in America" also highlighted new artists who, at the time, were relatively unknown, including Cheryll Leo-Gwin, who later designed a piece at the side entrance of the Museum's earlier location on 7th Avenue, Art Louie, Steve Momii, Amy Nikaitani, Tommie T. Oiye and Dean Wong.

To further expand I.D. art, I operated an art gallery in our architectural office space. I also donated gallery space for the Western Washington University's Center for Urban Studies for a class that Barry Mar taught and for ikebana lessons taught by Nobie Chan's mother, Madam Kodama. I volunteered at Cicada, a small arts and crafts co-op that Diana Bowers,

Pioneer Square Merchants Association, 1973 – Author's photo.

Mayumi Tsutakawa and other community members ran for a number of years in the International District. I coordinated holiday craft fairs in the District and, of course, helped out the Wing Luke Asian Museum whenever they needed a hand.

In the 1970s, Asian American leaders got involved in electoral politics as another route to community change and empowerment. Because we had a house that was centrally located and suitable for large gatherings, we hosted many of the early political fundraisers. Through the years, I found that a celebration where people can create a common social network is what cements successful community action.

Early grassroots political activists were Min Masuda, Don Kazama and Frank Fujii. They and a few others established an organization called Asian Americans for Political Action (AAPA). The group hosted political forums and made sure that local candidates addressed questions about affirmative action, bilingual education and preservation and development of the International District.

At the initial meetings, some of the spouses – Hana Masuda, Sally Kazama and Mich Fujii – wore Japanese aprons and prepared and served food for the participants. The role of

the women started shifting when Mich Fujii, who served as treasurer for a number of political campaigns, decided to step around to the other side of the table. She became one of the first Asian Americans appointed to a state board, serving on the State Board of Tax Appeals. Mich – along with Dolores Sibonga, who served on the Seattle City Council, and Ruby Chow, who was elected to the King County Council – helped paved the way. Asian American women have played key roles in the political arena ever since.

There were more setbacks than victories in the early years. We supported a lot of unsuccessful candidates. We got used to going to election night parties where less than ten people showed up at the candidate's house to lament over what a difference they could have made if only the candidate had won.

Joey, Ruth and Ben Woo in 1990
– Author's photo.

Things changed when Ruth Yoneyama Woo came on the scene. Considered the community's longtime political guru, Ruth began her political career as the receptionist for former Seattle Mayor Gordon Clinton, who served from 1956 to 1964. When Dan Evans was elected Governor in 1964, he asked her to come to Olympia. As the Governor's gregarious greeter and receptionist for eight years, she became a political power broker and respected confidante to governors and campaign workers alike.

Ruth does not discourage anyone with political ambition. Her skill is being a good listener and getting candidates to question themselves as to whether their desire to run for office is motivated by altruistic or self-serving reasons. Credited with working on and getting community volunteers for many successful political campaigns for both the Democratic and Republican parties, Ruth helped opened the community's access to politicians statewide.

After years of working on unsuccessful campaigns, AAPA finally backed a winner: Charles Royer, who became Seattle Mayor in 1978. I went with Jeanne Okimoto to the Royer election night party. We were both shocked at the mob scene. The hall was jam-packed with

television camera lights and campaigners waving signs that read: "Charlie, call me at xxx-xxxx!" Everyone wanted Royer to hire them for jobs and was pushing to get near the winner. We left to go to a Central Area election night party for a candidate who lost. I found it a lot more fun being with a handful of loyal friends than being in a room full of strangers and opportunists. Besides, there was better food and wine.

Mayor Charley Royer did not forget the support of the Asian Pacific American community, hiring Arlene Oki as community liaison. Ruth Woo began working for newly-elected City Attorney Doug Jewett. Ruth brought together Washington State Commission on Asian American Affairs Executive Director Diane Wong, Rita Elway, myself and others to lobby for an Asian appointment to fill a vacant seat on the Seattle City Council. Human rights attorney and former community newspaper editor Dolores Sibonga secured the appointment.

At one of the meetings, Gary Locke, working at the time as an attorney for the King County Prosecutor's Office, dropped by in his flannel shirt and jeans and expressed his interest in running for office. While others reacted with little enthusiasm, Ruth told him to give her a call. A few years later, we held Gary's first fundraiser at our house. Ruth Woo was his campaign manager. Gary served as State Representative for five terms, was chair of the powerful Ways and Means Committee, and went on become a popular two-term Governor. He appointed me to a seven-year term as one of three Washington State Liquor Control Board members. Ruth Woo declined his offer to work for him.

After Dolores Sibonga was appointed to the Seattle City Council, Rita Fujiki Elway served as her aide before moving on to work for Michael Hildt when he was elected on the Council. City Council member George Benson's respected legislative aide was Alan Kurimura. At the suggestion of Ruth Woo and perhaps because his wife Margo was a Garfield classmate of Fred Paulsell, City Council member Tim Hill hired me to work for him without an interview. Rita, Alan and I were the first Asian legislative aides on the Seattle City Council. Dolores served with distinction in her position for three terms and remains a political icon and mentor for the community today.

Our presence in City government added to the growing political clout of Asian Americans, enabling us to more effectively promote funding and support for community issues.

Soon after Dolores' appointment in 1978, Ruth Woo, Rita Fujiki Elway, Alan Kurimura and I were interviewed by the *Asian Family Affair* for a special issue titled, "Asians in City Hall." Editor Alan Sugiyama asked each of us whether we would ever run for office.

Rita told the newspaper that she anticipated "always being involved in politics to some extent." Alan, who now works with Uwajimaya's Tomio Moriguchi, said he was "absolutely positive" he would never run for political office because he did not want to give up his personal life. Typically self-effacing, Ruth, who is courted by candidates statewide, answered

Asian Family Affair, 1978.

that she too would never run for office. She added: "And I think people who volunteer for campaigns are crazier." I answered: "I couldn't get elected dogcatcher."

When Charley Royer was Mayor – he served three four-year terms, from 1978 to 1990 – the community enjoyed strong ties and access to City Hall. Many elected officials became personal friends and neighbors. In the 1970s, City Council member Michael Hildt was a Mt. Baker neighbor, as were fellow Council members John Miller and Phyllis Lamphere. I worked on Seattle City Council member Paul Kraabel's campaign. Joey and I often played bridge with the Kraabels. Tim Hill's twin sons and our son Jeff attended Broadview Elementary together because of the bussing program.

Council member Sam Smith, the first African American elected to the Council, always gave me a big hug and called me "neighbor" – knowing that I came from the Central Area and went to school with many of his constituents. He had difficulty remembering my name, but I have that same kind of problem of remembering names. Through my Mt. Baker Community Club activities and my work at Seattle Housing Authority, I also knew Council member Jeanette Williams and former King County Executive Randy Revelle.

Many elected officials still live in Mt. Baker, including King County Executive Ron Sims, former Mayor Norm Rice and former Seattle City Council member Jane Noland.

After a period of activism and aggressive lobbying of the City, many of us became fairly astute at figuring out how to "work" the system to ensure that it would be more responsive to Asian American community needs. We settled into positions on the boards of community agencies and learned how to move forward projects and build more lasting organizations.

In 1978, I became the first female president of the Inter*Im board. I had never conducted meetings before and it was an invaluable learning experience. This experience led to appointments to civic boards like the United Way executive board, where I served with Mary Gates, Bruce Nordstrom and Constance Rice. The board initiated the first Leadership Tomorrow program, which trains leaders for the Puget Sound region. I also served as the chair of the Seattle Center Foundation and Bumbershoot in 1980, the first year the event charged admission.

Longtime Inter*Im board members Tomio Moriguchi, Shigeko Uno, Ben Woo and Barry Mar provided the leadership to implement community projects. The City of Seattle hired James Mason as the first International District Manager. He was succeeded by Alan Kurimura. Their combination of talent, timing, and temperament resulted in the development of the International District into a neighborhood with a balance of mom-and-pop restaurants and shops, housing, professional offices and social services.

As ABCs know, it is important to have parties to celebrate accomplishments and success. Everyone looked forward to Inter*Im's annual holiday parties at Ed Burke's historic Nippon Kan Theatre building because of the mix of attendees and wonderful food. Shigeko Uno went to every I.D. restaurant to ask for donations of food, and Uwajimaya's Tomio Moriguchi could always be counted on to fill in the slack. It was one of a must-attend event for the Mayor and City Council members, and a coveted invitation for those involved in the I.D.

When Inter*Im was approaching its tenth year in 1979, we knew we needed to hold a special party. At the time of the anniversary, the *Seattle Weekly* had a "gang of four" – notable architects and urban designers – draw up a grand vision for the future of Seattle. Their "grand vision" would have impacted the International District. So we decided to develop our own plan. The International District 1980-2000 Master Plan was created by a group of us: architects Tom Kubota, Dennis Su, Ben Woo and myself. We revealed the plan at the anniversary dinner in front of Mayor Royer. The vision and predictions are amazingly close to what the District looks like today. The only error we made was in our prediction that Bob Santos would become Mayor of Seattle. Of course, many of us still regard "Uncle Bob" as the Mayor of the International District.

Inter*Im's 10th anniversary party was a big success. The Mayor and most of the Council members attended and were impressed by the I.D. Master Plan. Inter*Im was awarded funding for new projects through the SCIDPDA. We went to the City Council chambers to lobby for Community Development Block Grants funding to develop the Bush-Asia Center "Annex" project. This project involved the conversion of the old China Garage on 7th Avenue into a combined home for the Wing Luke Asian Museum and several community theater groups, including Northwest Asian American Theatre. Bea Kiyohara, the founding "mother" of Northwest Asian American Theatre (NWAAT), was instrumental in the lobbying efforts.

Council member Paul Kraabel took it on as his own personal crusade and the City stepped forward to support the project. Gary Locke and several other legislators secured major construction dollars from the state as well. Because of my strong personal interest in the arts, I felt that the completion of the "Annex" – securing a space for Wing Luke and for NWAAT – was an important building block in creating a balanced infrastructure to support the neighborhood. To me, these two arts projects were crowning jewels during the International District's golden period of community action.

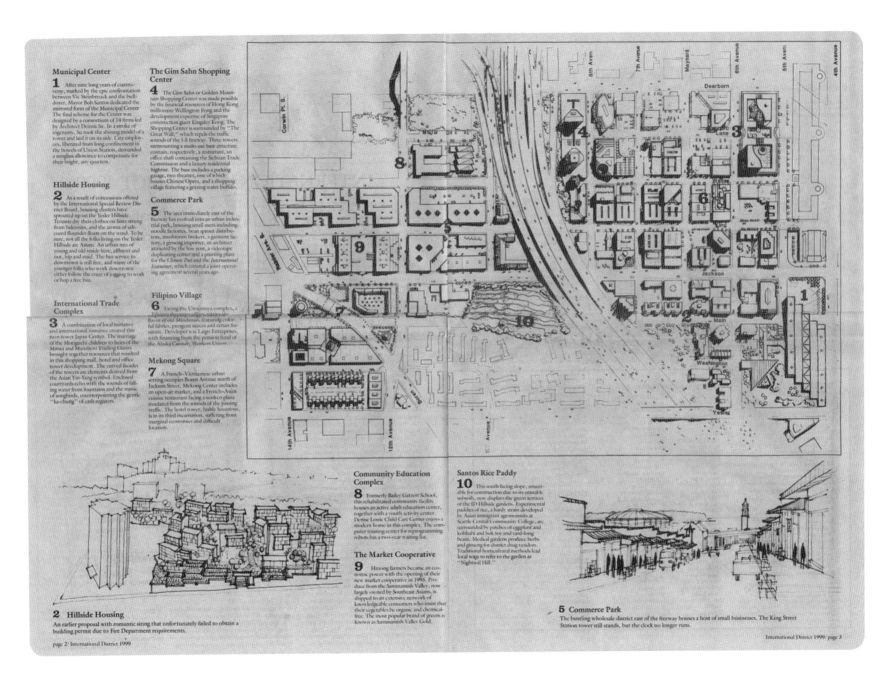

Municipal Center

1 After nine long years of controversy, marked by the epic confrontation between Vic Steinbrueck and the bulldozer, Mayor Bob Santos dedicated the mirrored form of the Municipal Center. The final scheme for the Center was designed by a consortium of 14 firms led by Architect Dennis Su. In a stroke of ingenuity, Su took the shining model of a tower and laid it on its side. City employees, liberated from long confinement in the bowels of Union Station, demanded a sunglass allowance to compensate for their bright, airy quarters.

Hillside Housing

2 As a result of concessions offered by the International Special Review District Board, housing clusters have sprouted up on the Yesler Hillside. Tenants dry their clothes on lines strung from balconies, and the aroma of salt-cured flounder floats on the wind. To be sure, not all the folks living on the Yesler Hillside are Asians. An urban mix of young and old reside here, affluent and not, hip and staid. The bus service to downtown is still free, and many of the younger folks who work downtown either follow the craze of jogging to work or hop a free bus.

International Trade Complex

3 A combination of local initiative and international romance created this twin tower Japan Center. The marriage of the Moriguchi children to heirs of the Mitsui and Marubeni Trading Giants brought together resources that resulted in this shopping mall, hotel and office tower development. The curved facades of the towers are elements derived from the Asian Yin-Yang symbol. Enclosed courtyards echo with the sounds of falling water from fountains and the music of songbirds, counterpointing the gentle "ka-ching" of cash registers.

The Gim Sahn Shopping Center

4 The Gim Sahn or Golden Mountain Shopping Center was made possible by the financial resources of Hong Kong millionaire Wellington Fong and the development expertise of Singapore construction giant Kingsley Kong. The Shopping Center is surrounded by "The Great Wall," which repels the traffic sounds of the I-5 freeway. Three towers surmounting a multi-use base structure contain, respectively, a restaurant, an office shaft containing the Sichuan Trade Commission and a luxury residential highrise. The base includes 4 parking garage, two theatres, one of which houses Chinese Opera, and a shopping village featuring a grazing water buffalo.

Commerce Park

5 The area immediately east of the freeway has evolved into an urban industrial park, housing small users including noodle factories, bean sprout distributors, mushroom brokers, a garment factory, a ginseng importer, an architect attracted by the low rent, a videotape duplicating center and a printing plant for the *Chinese Post* and the *International Examiner*, which entered a joint operating agreement several years ago.

Filipino Village

6 Facing the Uwajimaya complex, a Tagalog shopping gallery captures the flavor of old Mindanao, featuring colorful fabrics, pungent sauces and rattan furniture. Developer was Lapu Enterprises, with financing from the pension fund of the Alaska Cannery Workers Union.

Mekong Square

7 A French-Vietnamese urban setting occupies Boren Avenue north of Jackson Street. Mekong Center includes an open-air market, and a French-Asian cuisine restaurant facing a sunken plaza insulated from the sounds of the passing traffic. The hotel tower, lushly luxurious, is in its third incarnation, suffering from marginal economies and difficult location.

Community Education Complex

8 Formerly Bailey Gatzert School, this rehabilitated community facility houses an active adult education center, together with a youth activity center. Denise Louie Child Care Center enjoys a modern home in this complex. The computer training center for reprogramming robots has a two-year waiting list.

The Market Cooperative

9 Hmong farmers became an economic power with the opening of their new market cooperative in 1995. Produce from the Sammamish Valley, now largely owned by Southeast Asians, is shipped to an extensive network of knowledgable consumers who insist that their vegetables be organic and chemical-free. The most popular brand of greens is known as Sammamish Valley Gold.

Santos Rice Paddy

10 This south facing slope, unsuitable for construction due to its unstable subsoils, now displays the green terraces of the ID Hillside gardens. Experimental paddies of rice, a hardy strain developed by Asian immigrant agronomists at Seattle Central Community College, are surrounded by patches of eggplant and kohlrabi and bok choy and yard-long beans. Medical gardens produce herbs and ginseng for district drug vendors. Traditional horticultural methods lead local wags to refer to the garden as "Nightsoil Hill."

2 Hillside Housing
An earlier proposal with romantic siting that unfortunately failed to obtain a building permit due to Fire Department requirements.

5 Commerce Park
The bustling wholesale district east of the freeway houses a host of small businesses. The King Street Station tower still stands, but the clock no longer runs.

The International District Master Plan, published in the International Examiner *in 1983.*

Going for Gold

Running for Office

Going for Gold
Running for Office

Vera poses with Joel's high school classmates for a campaign photo – Yuen Lui photo.

By the early 1980s, I had thought about running for political office for years. Seeing first-hand what the public schools were like, I wanted to improve the education system for our three children. As a small business owner, I knew how vital the schools were to the health of the economy and wanted to provide tax relief to small businesses. And after volunteering for political campaigns without seeing any significant ABC appointments, I wanted to help change that situation.

Our three children went through public schools during the troubled 1960s. My neighbors and I had worked very hard to turn our neighborhood school into one that had a racially balanced student population and a quality education experience, only to have the efforts dismantled by the Seattle School District's desegregation and busing plan. Although our children maintained their community friends, many lost the advantages of creating lasting friendships within their own neighborhood. For some, the experience of being bused to school in another neighborhood opened opportunities to explore larger arenas. For less outgoing students, it reinforced divisions because childhood friends were separated and students from different communities didn't mix easily without having some common bond.

Instead of implementing a single solution, I felt that alternatives that promote or reward community and parental resources to strengthen the public education system within a neighborhood should have also been explored. The involvement of the Mt. Baker neighborhood in turning John Muir Elementary School around was a prime example.

At the Seattle Housing Authority (SHA), I saw how important it was for policymakers to include their constituents in the planning process. In 1974, I was in charge of the study to redevelop Yesler Terrace based on an old plan to tear down the existing buildings and build mixed income housing to replace them.

Yesler Terrace and other SHA low-income "garden communities" like Rainier Vista and Holly Park were built as military housing during World War II. Yesler Terrace is located on a hill between the International District and the Central Area and has spectacular views of Puget Sound and downtown. By the time of the study, these housing structures were badly deteriorated. Many returning ABC veterans like Dr. Eugene Ko had lived in Yesler Terrace after they returned from World War II and had married their sweethearts.

The Seattle Housing Authority did not ask for input from the residents prior to the management team's decision. We hired the architectural firms of NBBJ and a minority-owned subcontractor Arai Jackson to update and implement the retrofit.

At the first community meeting, Harry Thomas, at that time the executive director of Neighborhood House and the resident council president, made it clear that he and others intended to fight the plan to tear down their community. Eventually, we reached a compromise. Instead of tearing down Yesler Terrace, it was rehabilitated and modernized, complete with wood parquet floors that architect Jerry Arai insisted be installed. Twenty years later, Harry Thomas became the executive director of Seattle Housing Authority and oversaw comprehensive redevelopment of other SHA "garden communities" at Rainier and Holly Park. Sometimes, it takes the right person and the right timing to implement change.

That experience gave me a healthy respect for the importance of the public process. With the support of the management, the residents participated in future SHA projects. As a result, the public housing residents were in SHA's corner when it decided to tear down Greenwood Gardens, a crime-ridden housing complex located in Rainier Vista in Southeast Seattle. The huge building with long corridors was poorly designed for residents' safety. By working together, the residents and SHA were able to get Community Development Block Grants and do long-range planning and fund social services in these garden communities.

At the Seattle Housing Authority, I also saw insensitivity. SHA was in charge of the low- and no-interest loans for the Mt. Baker Neighborhood Rehabilitation Program. One activist neighbor had applied for a loan. The project manager showed me his application and said, "He's an architect! I've seen his tastefully decorated house. He doesn't qualify for a loan." I told him that he was an architecture classmate of Joey and I knew for a fact that this applicant was struggling in his practice. He was able to make his home look nice because of his taste and creativity, not because he had money. He had hand built his furnishings and had bought a $50 silkscreen for his wife from my gallery after I agreed that he could pay it off in monthly payments of five dollars. Like the other executives, this SHA official wasn't a bad person, just thoughtless at times. Seeing what had happened at SHA, I realized the importance of having a leader who could promote greater sensitivity. That was the first time I thought about running for office.

After leaving SHA, I worked as a legislative aide to Seattle Council member Tim Hill, who hired me on the recommendation of Ruth Woo. Tim was the best boss I ever worked for. Like my Mt. Baker neighbors, he was very supportive and wanted me to succeed. He took the time to sit down and explain what he expected from his staff. He was open to my invitations to visit the I.D. Years later, he supported me in my bid for office, even though he was a Republican. Although he received high praise while in office, Tim received bad press when he retired because he wanted to work a few more months to get a full pension. He was a dedicated public servant who deserved better, but the reality is that the press and the public can be very fickle.

Tim Hill was part of a new emerging wave of centrist politicians of the 1960s and '70s. This group – which included City Attorney Doug Jewett and Seattle City members John Miller and Paul Kraabel – believed in "clean and open" government. They were sympathetic to the viewpoint of businesses, yet open to addressing the inequalities of race and class. Both Democrats and Republicans would do well now to learn from that group of non-partisan elected officials.

I compare Tim Hill to Jimmy Carter in that both were "process-oriented" people, interested in listening to all sides rather than charging in with an unyielding stance. At our first meeting, Tim told me he only expected me to never embarrass him, to give him good press, and to keep up a comprehensive binder on issues. He wanted to know the fiscal and social impacts, options, and who would be upset or pleased if he took a specific stand. He studied each issue thoroughly and usually came into a committee meeting without anyone knowing how he might vote. He asked hard questions and weighed each decision carefully before acting.

In 1979, Tim was the budget chair and I was his committee clerk. It was a tremendous test for me, especially since the League of Women Voters planned to shadow me through the budget process and make a report. Luckily, Council member George Benson's aide Alan Kurimura and Council's Budget Analyst Peter Moy took me under their wing. It seemed that every department had a different way of presenting their budget request. I reviewed each department's request using the same criteria: past performance, percentage of budget, and projections of return and long-term benefits. Tom Ko checked my figures with his manual adding machine on our kitchen table. Because the budget did not pass till after Thanksgiving, Joey had to take the family to our annual Honolulu vacation without me. But the League of Women Voters gave a glowing report.

Later, after Tim moved on and was elected King County Executive in 1986, I interviewed for the position of King County Clerk. During the interview, he asked me, "What would you do if I told you to do something that you did not believe in or knew that was wrong?" I answered that would never be a problem because I knew he would never do something dishonest. " He gave me the kind of look that a teacher does when you give the wrong answer. I realized later that Tim's question was about ethics and that I should have responded by saying that I would never act contrary to what I knew was right. He didn't hire me.

The Seattle City Council is supposed to be non-partisan. Throughout the budget review, Tim's colleagues – Dolores Sibonga, Sam Smith, George Benson, Paul Kraabel, John Miller, Jeanette Williams and Randy Revelle – had an attitude of mutual respect. The Republicans – Tim, Paul and John – were more conservative than the Democrats – Dolores and Sam – but all of them were able to work together. It was collective leadership, and to me, it was public policymaking at its best. I thought again about running for office.

I learned about partisan politics when I asked State Representative John Eng for an appointment to the Democratic Caucus so I could explore the possibility of becoming a candidate. It was during the 1981 legislative session when the Republicans were in the majority. Because I was concerned that the inner city needs would be overlooked in a Republican pro-business session, I asked to work on the Human Services Committee. They assigned me to be a committee clerk, which meant I spent most of the session at the copy machine. I found that partisan politics often had nothing to do with compromise. The Republican chair of the human services committee did not review any requests from community organizations, rarely spent any time studying issues and had already made up his mind to cut funding according to the recommendations of the party leadership. In my view, this was a scary way to make public policy.

The bright spot for me was carpooling to and from Olympia with Teresita Batayola, Tony Lee and Gary Locke, who worked for Ways and Means Chair Jim McDermott. During those long commutes, I often served as a sounding board for Gary Locke when he was going through a personal crisis. After discussions with Ruth Woo, Gary finally made the decision to run for State Representative in 1982. We kicked off his campaign at our house, with his father barbecuing delicious salmon in our driveway.

After the session, I applied for several appointments without success. With three children in college, I needed a job. Even though Joey and I appeared to be doing well, his practice was always a struggle. Everyone appreciated Joey's pro bono architectural services when developing funding proposals for community projects, but the architectural contracts were usually awarded to an outside firm. It was the same for me when I applied for jobs in the I.D. where I had volunteered for years. In communities where everyone has known each other since childhood, it seems that you sometimes have to work even harder to be taken seriously on a professional level.

Joey and I didn't let rejections get us down because many of our ABC friends were in the same boat. There are still many struggling mom-and-pop small business owners in our community today. However, through community networks, we have been able to maintain a good quality of life. As ABC small business owners know, bringing in a modest income doesn't affect your community standing. Everyone is given an equal measure of respect in the community's athletic,

Campaign meeting at the Ing house. From left: Constance Rice, Jeanne Okimoto, Jim Webert and Shigeko Uno – Author's photo.

church and nonprofit organizations. It didn't matter whether you were a plumber, electrician, postman or a physician.

Once my daughter JaDeane said to me, "Mom, I never thought that we were poor when we were growing up. I thought you were just cheap!" I smiled, remembering the early days of Joey's practice, when he was supporting the family on a shoestring and we couldn't afford to send her to private school even though she was afraid to go to the neighborhood school. But it felt good to know we managed to give our children a sense of security and the feeling that they were never deprived.

I decided to run for State Representative in the 37th District while playing bridge with Ben and Ruth Woo on a snowy Sunday morning. Ben, Council member Paul Kraabel, Joey and I had to turn back from our trip to the ski slopes because of a severe snowstorm. While Ben and Joey were busy trying to dig the car out of the snow and get moving again, Paul was going from car to car to offer words of encouragement to other drivers who were stuck on the road just like us. He made folks feel that he took a personal interest in their safety. That is another important responsibility of a good politician.

We managed to get the car free and drove back to the Woos' before lunch. Ruth was surprised to see us. When Paul left, I suggested making the best of our Sunday outing by playing bridge. Ruth and I usually play "political" bridge, meaning we're more interested in talking about upcoming campaigns and issues than engaging in actual card playing. We talked about the

Keeping it to the point, 1984 campaign – Dean Wong photo.

need to have more people of color run for office. After bidding my favorite 3 no trump contract, I announced that I wouldn't mind running for office. There was stunned silence.

Ruth heard me out. Then she called Representative Gary Locke and asked him to come over. Gary came right away, probably thinking that he was getting another last minute invitation to a dinner cooked by Ben. Gary asked me why I wanted to run. It was the first opportunity to verbalize what I had been thinking about for years: "To work for excellence in public education, support small business enterprises, and provide job training and public safety for our district." He responded positively, then asked, "When do we eat?"

Before making the final decision, I contacted my trusted sounding boards. After talking it through with my closest I.D. friend Alan Kurimura, he told Ruth he had never seen me more confidant. It was another acid test when *International Examiner* editor Ron Chew called to interview me because I felt that he would be able to see through any bull. Their support made me feel that I was a credible candidate.

Ruth, who served as my campaign manager, gave me a list of people to call to secure endorsements. It was a Who's Who listing of the Democratic powerbrokers, most of whom I did not know personally. But it turned out that all of them were very open to speaking to me because of Ruth. I secured the support of nearly all of them. One of the most memorable meetings was with attorney Charles Goldmark, someone who was always willing to support new up-and-coming candidates. He was very welcoming and gave me his endorsement. His openness, however, led to an unthinkable tragedy for him and his entire family. The year after my campaign, he opened his door to a stranger on Christmas Eve. This deranged person killed Charles, his wife and two sons because he believed, mistakenly, that Charles was Jewish and a Communist.

Joey, who took up the responsibility for my campaign yard signs, rented Ben's architectural office in Mt. Baker so he could be closer to our home campaign headquarters. My sister Helen's mother-in-law, Margaret Gojio, who was also Joey's administrator, was the campaign treasurer. Larry Gojio designed my campaign logo, and Ben Woo created the silk screen for my yard signs. Co-chairs were Constance Rice, Yvonne Banks and Dr. Eugene Ko. Ruth managed the campaign strategy. One of Joey's urban design students Rita Romero volunteered as campaign manager. Ruth also found Jay Jagod who enthusiastically escorted me to all functions and made sure I completed my daily doorbelling assignments. No one was paid, but Joey kept everyone happy by keeping a steady supply of his homemade bread around.

The campaign team was set; now all we needed was to groom me to be a credible candidate. The incumbent John O'Brien had been in office for 42 years. The other challenger, who had lost in earlier matchup against O'Brien, was running again. Still, I felt I had a fighting chance with Ruth's help.

Joey and son Joel took up their job of putting up yard signs with great enthusiasm. There were signs at every house on our block, on the block above us, on the hill below our house, and up the hill to Beacon Hill. It was an awesome sight and I got my first inkling of how powerful recognition could be. Rita Romero remarked: "It's going to be hard going from being the center of attention to be an ordinary person again." Political power can be seductive, but with family, friends and community around to put me in my place, it was never a problem.

Suddenly, the yard signs started disappearing, even from the yards of personal friends. Someone was taking them down as fast as Joey and Joel could put them up. Joey found the lost signs in the other challenger's yard. Hopping mad, he considered calling the press. However, the campaign staff didn't want to start negative campaigning or compromise personal integrity. But it was eye-opening to find out that some candidates will do anything to win. Being a candidate takes a thick skin. That summer, I endured the stealing of yard signs, being hurt by friends who were dear to me, negative campaigning and having an awful lot of doors slammed in my face.

Running for office was also gratifying and humbling. Thanks to the support of Assunta Ng, who published the

Northwest Asian Weekly and *Seattle Chinese Post*, hundreds of "non-political" ABCs contributed money and volunteered on my campaign. I think it was because they could identify with me and wanted to help elect the first Chinese American woman to statewide office. I was so appreciative of their support that I stayed up nights worrying that I might let them down. It was no longer a personal campaign, but a community-driven one.

Ruth arranged for mock interview sessions with seasoned political campaign volunteers and officials. I was awful. It is one thing to feel empathy, but being able to articulate viewpoints and develop realistic solutions is much more difficult. Ruth asked Joey to rub his eyes if I was taking too long to answer their questions. I wanted to let my friends around the table know that I had done my homework and went on and on while looking down at my notes. Had I looked up, I would have seen Joey rubbing his eyes like crazy and the interviewers bored to tears. Gary Locke said, "Up or down? Are you for the issue or not? That's all anyone wants to know." I believe what he really wanted to say was, "Keep it simple, stupid."

I joined Toastmasters, which helped correct my "ums" and "ahs" after every sentence and reminded me that the attention span of most people is under one minute. Political consultant Mike Shadow tutored me on how to make eye contact and hand gestures. I learned to make a point within the first sentence, repeat it by the middle of the speech, then repeat it at the end.

The Municipal League, which interviews all candidates, gave me a rating of "Very Good," one step from the highest ranking of "Excellent." The other challenger got a ranking of Excellent, the incumbent got a rating of "Good." I secured endorsements from City Council members Dolores Sibonga, Virginia Galle, Paul Kraabel and Norm Rice, the King County Women's Political Caucus, Washington State Chapter of the National Organization for Women, Asian Pacific Women's Caucus and Filipino-American Political Action Group of Washington. However, because of lack of name familiarity outside the community, I did not get a major newspaper endorsement. The *Seattle Weekly* didn't even bother to interview me before they endorsed the other challenger. I also realized that most of my supporters did not live in the 37th District or were not registered voters. The votes were pretty evenly split. There were about 1,000 votes separating the three candidates. I came in a close third. The incumbent won.

Endorsements in a campaign mailer – Author's collection.

Even though I lost the race, I took pride in the integrity of the campaign and was heartened by the best wishes of many community friends and supportive community paper editorials. The challenger immediately moved out of the modest house he lived in during the campaign. Being from a wealthy family, he may have moved there just to qualify to represent the District. John O'Brien, who won another term in the legislature, invited me to his annual St. Patrick's Day party. After he retired, his colleagues named the Legislative Building after him.

After my campaign, I had a severe bout of Asian guilt. My sister Helen tried to snap me out of it by curtly declaring, "Why don't you just take out an ad and say, 'I'm sorry.'" I felt I had failed those whom I respected. I felt I had failed all my community aunties and uncles, and those who had contributed to my campaign, some of whom were of modest means. In the midst of this guilt, I remembered Ah Ba's words: "Find a way to make good for every bad thing that happens to you."

In 1985, a year after my campaign, I opened the Prima Vera Gallery Café. I told Joey that it would be a win-win situation. With a restaurant, I would never have to cook. I would only open for breakfast and lunch and still be able to work in the architectural office in the afternoon. We could hire a cook and eat the leftovers. Joey's older widowed sister Bebe would prepare her wonderful carrot cake. I would make the café available for rent for community and political fundraisers at night.

My great idea about hiring a surrogate cook turned out to be a pipe dream because we weren't making enough money to keep one. So I – who didn't cook because Ah Ma was one of the best – did the cooking and cashiering as well as the cleaning of the toilets. I could only afford one minimum wage employee who bused, washed dishes and cleaned. Just as we had donated our professional design services pro bono to community organizations, I was donating the space to favored candidates or community organizations once again.

Excerpt from a restaurant guide – Author's collection.

Most of the customers came in for coffee and carrot cake. I usually would have only one customer at a time coming in, so it was okay. But I would be swamped whenever six or more came in together at the same time. I enjoyed the daily visits of nearby KOMO-TV personalities and union leaders who spent $2 a piece on a slice of Auntie Bebe's carrot cake and coffee. Most of the candidates who used my space for fundraisers won. One was King County Council member Larry Phillips, who hired my waitress to be his legislative aide and my sister Mari to be his administrative assistant.

I shall always be grateful to the restaurant critic who came in and never printed a review, but instead had me written up in the tourist book on Seattle's restaurants. I operated Prima Vera for five years, never taking home a salary. In 2008, we started to donate the space to three Asian theater groups – ReACT, SIS Productions, and Pork-filled Players – for their rehearsals.

With the support of editor Ron Chew, I started a weekly column called "Dim Sum: Bits of the Asian American dream" in the *International Examiner* in 1988. I wrote about growing up in Chinatown, Seattle's International District and Asian Pacific pioneers, newcomers and notables. After Ron left the *Examiner*, Assunta Ng picked up my column for the *Northwest Asian Weekly*. I did weekly columns for Assunta for five years. Vancouver's *Chinatown News* magazine, circulated throughout North America, printed my old columns after I stopped writing.

Several years later, there was an open State Senate seat in my district. Ruth told me that political consultant Blair Butterworth mentioned that his firm wouldn't mind donating its services if I considered running for the position. The familiar knot in the stomach came back. I declined, although I felt I would have been

Prima Vera Gallery Cafe
112 Fifth Ave. N.
441-8372

Mon-Fri: 8:30 am to 3:00 pm
Sat-Sun: Closed
No Reservations
No Credit Cards
Beer and Wine
Outdoor Seating

An informal cafe in elegant surroundings, the Prima Vera came about in an odd way. After renting the spot several times to unsuccessful tenants, architects and urban planners Vera Ing and her husband decided they could do better. They built a true art gallery with well-lighted paintings, added some tables and folding chairs under colorful umbrellas, a high-tech bar, a baby grand piano and magazines for atmosphere, and created an informal cafe which just happens to be across from KOMO-TV and Radio and its over three hundred employees. "A pleasant surprise," says Vera.

She is one of those do-everything people who make the rest of us seem like we're just lounging around. When she ran for state representative in 1984, she needed a larger brochure just to list her credits; Vera holds so many titles and sits on so many boards you wonder if she has time to exercise. But she can also cook (her parents ran one of the first Chinese cafes in the International District), and every afternoon offers light lunches for the working crowd. Aside from soups and sandwiches she offers a few specials such as Pasta Prima Vera, pasta with sauteed vegetables in a cream sauce and a French pastry stuffed with salmon and peas or chicken and vegetables. Breakfast is continental.

In off hours, Vera can be found at her desk doing architectural work, or more often than not chatting at a back table with some of the most powerful ladies in the city. You don't order a Power Lunch at Vera's; it's already here.

a strong candidate for the open seat. I did not want to ask my community uncles and aunties for money again.

Although I did not succeed in my race, I feel my campaign was a privilege and that it opened many doors for other community candidates. Sometimes I hear people say that all politicians are crooked or worthless. I strongly disagree. Politics is a honorable calling. Getting involved is the only way to maintain our democracy and to make sure that we're fairly represented. I commend those who want to run for office for the right reasons.

During the campaign I learned several important lessons: 1) Run for office with conviction; 2) Believe you can make a difference; 3) Keep your solutions simple; 4) Power can be dangerously seductive; 5) Maintain your network of friends and family.

I remember attending a Martin Luther King, Jr. Day celebration where former Seattle Mayor Norm Rice, my Mt. Baker neighbor, implored the audience to think about the need to develop "collective leadership" rather than looking for individual leaders. His remarks were right on target. Collective and cooperative leadership is what it takes to move the ABC and Asian Pacific American community forward.

Golden Memories

Community Holidays and Traditions

Golden Memories
Community Holidays and Traditions

Campaign photo with Joel's high school classmates – Yuen Lui photo.

As my husband and I approach our golden wedding anniversary, I can't help but think about how lucky we have been. We've had a lot of ups and downs in our marriage, but what has sustained us through it all are our many friends, a supportive community and church, a loving family and treasured grandchildren.

Being active in the ABC network and the Mt. Baker community, Joey and I have often had to call a truce to our differences just so that we could amicably attend a milestone celebration. During the occasion of our 20th anniversary, Joey and I didn't feel much like partying because of serious marital difficulties. Joey had made some financial investments that had gone bad, creating major tensions in our relationship. We decided to mark the anniversary by having a few friends – the Okimotos and Washburns – over to our place. At one point in the evening, Dexter Washburn said, "There are some marriages, like national monuments, that must be preserved." Joey and I knew that his comment was directed at us. Our daughter JaDeane also made a comment when I was angry at her father: "Why are you so tough on Dad? He's a saint!" That's when I realized that breaking up with Joey also would mean breaking up the family.

Nothing binds the ABC community and Asian American families together like a celebration. And nothing makes a celebration more memorable than the food that's served.

Births, birthdays, holidays, graduations and other milestones are marked by the presence of traditional Chinese dishes and special foods.

It was usually up to the community mothers to prepare the dishes and remind us of the significance of special holidays. I wonder if they knew that by preserving these traditions, they probably saved many marriages or at least provided an excuse for a truce among troubled partners who had to attend the celebrations together rather than be subjected to unwanted questioning as to why their spouses weren't with them.

For Chinese New Year, community mothers prepared special dishes which symbolized wealth, longevity, promotion, success and good tidings for the coming year. Our community mothers chose sweet oranges, ordered Virginia ham and live chickens. They shopped for dried algae, fungi and oysters. They made *nian gao*, the Chinese New Year pudding cake made of sticky rice and brown sugar topped with red dates and sesame seeds, representing family unity. Our community mothers filled wooden New Year boxes with watermelon seeds (many children), candied carrots (wealth), coconut (good relationship between father and son), melons (descendants), lotus roots (friendship), and kumquats (blessings/luck).

Ah Ma boiled a whole chicken to put in front of Ah Ba's headstone and his picture in the living room during *Ching Ming*, the annual "tomb sweeping" celebration, usually occurring around April 5. During the Dragon Boat Festival, on the fifth day of the 5th month of the lunar calendar, Ah Ma would prepare *doong tai*, the sticky rice bundles filled with salted egg, Chinese sausage, dried shrimp, chestnuts, and peanuts wrapped in lotus leaves. Our house would be filled with steam and comfort food smells as I helped roll out the *cheong fun* (rice noodle roll) dough on her antique machinery. During the Mid-Autumn Festival, we would get moon cakes, a round delicacy filled with lotus seed paste and salted duck egg yolk. The truth is that I never cared for moon cakes.

An important holiday for overseas Chinese takes place on October 10. We call it Double Ten Day, marking the uprising on October 10, 1911 which led to the overthrow of the Manchu Dynasty, and the establishment of the modern Chinese republic. In the old days, parades were held in Chinatowns throughout the U.S. to mark the historic occasion.

In Seattle, the flag of Taiwan would be raised and there would be endless banquets, entertainment and speeches by Chinatown and Taiwan dignitaries at the Chong Wa Benevolent Association, across the street from our family's Don Ting Café.

The community mothers were in charge of carrying on the traditions and preparing the feasts. We Chinatown brats looked forward to the treats of the holiday, never thinking that one day it would fall on our shoulders to carry on the traditions. As we became mothers and grandmothers ourselves, we felt a renewed interest in passing some of these longstanding traditions onto our children.

Of course, the world has changed. In Ah Ma's day, our community mothers were homemakers, garment workers, shopkeepers, waitresses and laundry workers. With new opportunities, the community has become more diverse and affluent, and the food and traditions have changed. Thanks to the influx of new immigrants, there are Asian community markets and restaurants where we can buy the *nian gao, doong tai, cheong fun* and *jai,* the vegetarian monk's dish served for New Year. We no longer have to spend weeks gathering the ingredients and preparing and cooking these special foods from scratch.

Maybe some of us don't know – or remember – how to prepare some of these foods, but we now have the convenience of finding these familiar foods in Asian stores if we want to bring them back into our lives. When we eat these foods, it's the perfect time to share them with family and friends. The bond of sharing a meal together to mark a holiday or milestone is still the glue that holds together the community and the family.

Today's community mothers play bridge or golf instead of mah jong. They are administrators, college graduates, executives, professionals, property managers, consultants, government officials, politicians and teachers. They've moved beyond Chinatown and the inner-city

Norm Rice at Vera's 40th birthday party, 1980 – Author's photo.

neighborhoods into suburbia and into neighborhoods in towns and cities outside of Seattle.

As newlyweds, Joey and I would enjoy spending an evening at the home of Bob and Janice Wong. The men would give each other haircuts, and this would be followed by a home-cooked dinner and bridge. Jan was a travel agent and Bob was Joey's architecture classmate and a furniture maker. Their stylish home reflected Bob's design talents, and the dinner table was graced by Jan's flair for preparation. Jan was a terrific cook, and her dinners looked like the pictures in *Sunset Magazine*. She was always game to try any recipe once. She was also a very gregarious and generous host. When they moved back to Hawaii, we stayed at their home overlooking the ocean every year. We were among her many houseguests from around the world. Jan was a true community mother.

Jan and I started a women's bridge group in the 1960s. The group still plays once a month. The original bridge group was myself, Janice Wong, Carol Locke (who was King County Executive Gary Locke's administrator) Helen Kay (long-time president of the Wing Luke Asian Museum), Delores Dong, May Eng, Nina Eng and Neta Ding. My sister, Mari Eng, took Janice's place when she moved back to Hawaii. Neta's mother played mah jong with my mother and remembered going to my month-old baby party banquet as a teenager. This means I have been connected to Neta's family since birth. While I don't play with them now, I still enjoy being an alternative whenever I can so I can catch up with news about my lifelong friends.

The best part of the bridge night would be the great comfort food of my mother's time that many of the women knew how to make. Many of them preserved their recipes in the Seattle Chinese Community Girls Drill Team cookbooks. The cookbooks play a major part in maintaining Seattle's Toisanese history and traditions. Other Asian communities have done the same through church cookbooks. It is a delicious way to pass down traditions.

As our community's celebrations become increasingly pan-Asian Pacific, the foods from many different cultures are featured at community

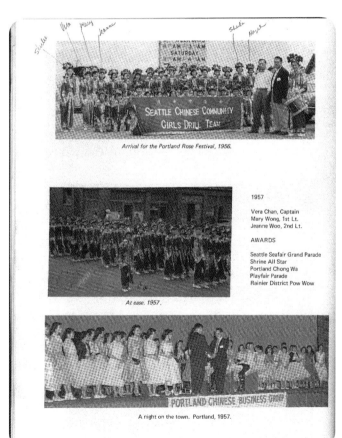

Arrival for the Portland Rose Festival, 1956.

1957

Vera Chan, Captain
Mary Wong, 1st Lt.
Jeanne Woo, 2nd Lt.

AWARDS

Seattle Seafair Grand Parade
Shrine All Star
Portland Chong Wa
Playfair Parade
Rainier District Pow Wow

At ease. 1957.

A night on the town. Portland, 1957.

events. When Joey and I attended the Wing Luke's Asian Museum's 2008 holiday party hosted by Mar-Pac Construction, the firm that remodeled the new historic building into a museum, the buffet and entertainment there was Hawaiian. Before the party we spent the afternoon with the bridge group where the snacks included sushi, teriyaki, and dim sum.

In Seattle, it was relatively easy for someone like me to transition from being a Chinatown brat to becoming a friend or colleague of the community mothers. Anne Chinn Wing was the community mother who took care of us during the preparations for my father's funeral in 1948. Anne and I later became colleagues and friends through bridge and participation in the Chinatown events like tours of the family associations during Chinese New Year, and the Chinatown Night and Parade during the Seattle Seafair celebrations in the 1950s, Moon Festival, and the Chinatown Chamber of Commerce queen pageant. Ruth Chinn and Helen Kay would take out precious heirloom gowns to wear for Chinese fashion shows to celebrate our rich heritage. Community mothers like Anne, Ruby Chow and Vi Mar would attend to important details of the celebrations, working closely with early Chinatown Chamber of Commerce leaders like Chin Han, Dr. Henry Luke and Abe Lum.

Ruth Chinn was one of the nicest community mothers. I always felt she was the unsung heroine of the Chinese community. Ruth's kindness and support was there for me at Chinese Baptist Church when I attended as a ragamuffin child. As Chinese Girl Scouts leader, she encouraged me to write an essay for a scholarship to the Girl Scouts camp. That was a favorite childhood experience. The 1958 Chinese College Students Christmas party at Ruth's house is where I reconnected with my future husband, six months after first meeting Joey at the wedding of Auntie Florence's daughter and breaking up with the boyfriend I had almost married. Two other couples started their courtship at that year's party: Sula and Joe Louie, and Pauline and Wayne Chin.

Moon Festival Committee at Ruby Chow's home, 1963 – Author's photo.

Garfield class reunion, 1993 – Author's photo.

Ruth and her husband Robert Chinn came from distinguished pioneer families and had college degrees from China. Like most early ABCs, Bob was unable to find gainful employment outside the community. Ruth, who published a Chinese community newsletter, helped give us a boost by publicizing Joey's architectural practice as it was getting off the ground. Ruth knew the skeletons in the ABC families, but tactfully kept them there. She once told me that she considered adopting my kid sister Helen herself before my own mother did. She gave our children their Chinese names, which I kept forgetting until she had me write them down in our wedding album. Later, when we were both volunteering for the Wing Luke Museum, I remember taking trips with her and discovering how much she relished good food. She would always came home with boxes of goodies for her family.

Ruth was not motivated by money, but rather by the desire to preserve tradition and give a boost to others. In 1960, Ruth and her husband Robert, who spent many years as a postman, established the first ABC savings and loan institution in Seattle, the United Savings and Loan Bank. When Joey and I married, she advised me to always save at least 10 percent of our earnings, wise advice that has served me well over the years. In 2003, United Savings and Loan Bank was sold to Washington Federal Savings Bank for $65 million. Ruth passed away in 2007 at the age of 92 in the same Beacon Hill home where I reconnected with Joey.

In communities like ours, it is often the women who provide the sense of culture, elegance and refinement for their families. One of the community mothers I looked up to as a model of class and style was Mimi Luke, the wife of Dr. Henry Luke, Chinatown's physician. Mimi was from New York, beautiful and always perfectly outfitted in *cheongsam*. It was hard for ABCs to establish a practice outside of Chinatown in those days. Community doctors were probably paid very little because of their immigrant client base. Dr. Luke's office was a tiny house overlooking the Chinese school playfield. Mimi's style and class added credibility to Dr. Luke's practice and enhanced how people viewed him. Other distinguished matriarchs were Mrs. Mon Wai from the Golden Wheel Restaurant in Yakima, Mrs. Chin Han from Chinatown's Four Seas Restaurant and Rose Louie, wife of George Louie, owner of Louie's Cuisine of China in Ballard.

In junior high and high school, the community mothers were the mothers of my friends. At Washington Junior High, one of my best friends was Linda Maekawa. Her parents owned a grocery store a block from school, on 18th Avenue and Jackson. They lived above the store. I usually spent the afternoons at Linda's. Her *obachan* (grandmother) always had a bowl of rice warmed with popcorn tea waiting for us. Hannah Maekawa, Linda's mother, was very stylish. She worked at the Frederick & Nelson department store downtown and often brought home cashmere sweater sets for Linda. She was also a great seamstress and made beautiful prom dresses for her daughter. As a result, Linda was the best dressed of all my friends.

I was the first lieutenant of the Seattle Chinese Community Girls Drill Team during its first out-of-town parade in Portland, Oregon in 1955. Needing a special dress, I bought three yards of polished polka-dotted fabric at Fusion's Fabric Store on Jackson for a dollar, and asked Hannah Maekawa if she would help me cut out the pattern pieces. Linda and I went over to her house after school to start the project. By then, Hannah had already finished sewing up the entire dress! The picture of me in that $1 spaghetti-strap dress has been in every reunion program of the Chinese Community Girls Drill Team.

Hannah was also influential in stopping me from making a ruinous life decision. At that time, my boyfriend was an ABC gambler from Portland that my mother did not approve of. I wasn't madly in love with him, but because of my mother's disapproval, I hung on out of pride and defiance. My mother had people checking up on me while she was at work. I had my girlfriends' dates pick me up at home to drive me to meet him. I had my mail sent to the Maekawa's house. It was a terrible way to spend the last semester of high school.

This boyfriend wanted to marry me and to move back to his hometown in the Midwest after my high school graduation and my trip to Hong Kong with Ah Ma. While I was in Hong

DOUBLE CELEBRATION

It was a double celebration for this couple, Pvt. William Chinn and his bride of a week, the former Dorothy Moe. They were honored at a wedding reception at the Twin Dragons, the largest private V-J Day party in Seattle's Chinatown.

Dorothy and William Chin
celebrate their wedding.

Kong, I even had a "wedding dress" made. In Hong Kong, we visited with Ah Ma's relatives and I saw the poverty which drove Ah Ma to America, seeking a better life. I came home with a deeper appreciation for the struggles of my immigrant parents.

When I returned to Seattle, there was a letter from this boyfriend waiting for me at the Maekawa house, along with a train ticket and news that his parents approved of our marriage. I panicked. For me, it was no longer a teenage grab for independence. This was about leaving my family and friends for good. Because I knew Hannah would not lecture me, I confided in her what was going on. She listened patiently until I talked myself out of marrying so young. I did not respond to a follow-up letter from him, in which he chided me and accused me of backing down because of my mother. I'm not sure Hannah realized what a profound impact she made on my future by just being a good listener.

The daughters and daughters-in-law of the Chin Han clan represented the kind of family unit I hoped to nurture for my own children. The family lived on the same block as their cousins Joanne and Virginia Chinn, my childhood friends. It was a large active family that managed to get together every weekend at their parents' home despite busy schedules and careers. Daughter Isabelle Chin was advisor to the Chi-ettes, the first ABC girls social club. Norma Ko set the standard for gracious living. Carol Chin helped Joanne and Virginia with make-up and dresses for our first proms. Helen Chin Lum was the advisor to the Girls Club which Joanne and Virginia Chinn and I started. Helen was also our wedding coordinator.

The men in the Chin Han family were also very influential in building the community network. In the 1960s, Wilbur and Abe built the successful Four Seas Restaurant on 8th Avenue and South King Street on a site that formerly served as Mrs. Chin Han's vegetable patch. Sons and sons-in-law Dentist William Chin, Wilbur Chin, Dr. Eugene "Curly" Ko and

New Year's Eve gathering with
Vancouver friends, 2000
– Author's photo.

Abe Lum helped establish or were charter members of the first Chinese Golf Club and ABC basketball leagues, which we joined after marriage. William's wife Dorothy was one of the earliest ABC women golfers. Being invited to Curly and Norma's Mt. Baker home for the hydroplane races or a Chinese Golf Club party was always a coveted treat.

Through the Cascade Golf Club and Seattle Chinese Athletic Association of the 1970s, I stayed connected with friends who had known me since Canton Alley, friends like Tom and Char Ko, Milt and Lil Lew, Frank and Diane Marr, Dan and Shirley Ko, Tuck and Dee Eng, and of course, my sister Mari Eng and husband Kai. During the ABC tri-cities tournaments in Portland, Vancouver, and Seattle, Joey and I met our Vancouver friends Al and Lena Lee, Bock and Kay Yip, Norm and Flo Chin, Yat and Shirley Yip, Ron and Lori Chong, Gerry and Merrilee Wong, and George and Sue Yen. The ABCs in both organizations are now in their seventies, and we have been the closest of friends since childhood. Although Joey and I have a wide range of friends, we feel privileged to have been part of these two tight circles.

These ABC friends have given us a strong sense of belonging. Together, we have attended three generations of family weddings, baby parties, anniversaries, birthdays and funerals. We have shared the joy of our successes, extended support to one another whenever we've fallen short of our goals, and we've readily forgiven each other's shortcomings and insensitivities. We have gone on joint family vacations, shared countless meals, celebrated milestones, and seen the birth of grandchildren. We have shared the best of times, and we have been there for one another during the worst of times, too.

I have been fortunate to have been part of several different communities that have nurtured family unity and neighborhood preservation. During the 1970s and 1980s, I was involved in the Mt. Baker neighborhood, International District and the Seattle Community College District.

In Mt. Baker, it was at the potlucks hosted by Community Club members where new residents like Joey and I began to build relationships and counter resentment over the new diversity that was "diluting" the neighborhood's "gold coast." Fred and Marsha Paulsell would invite their sons' classmates, who attended John Muir Elementary School, to come over to their home to participate in impromptu afternoon concerts, followed by spaghetti dinners served on fine china in the formal dining room. The parents of the other kids would be invited over, too. Twenty years after the Paulsells moved from Mt. Baker, we received an invitation to the wedding of Fred Paulsell Jr. at Marsha's waterfront home on Mercer Island.

Our sons' childhood memories include the many meals with their surrogate mothers in the house next door. For Joel, it was Dorothy Schroeder's home; for Jeff it was Virginia Washburn's place. Dorothy and Virginia enhanced the table manners and conversational skills of both Joel and Jeff.

By celebrating milestones with Mt. Baker friends like Virginia and Dexter Washburn and Joe and Jeanne Okimoto, we helped each other through our respective midlife crises and learned how to live our lives with balance and meaning. I will always remember the honor of being included in Jeannie and Joe's intimate family wedding, and the elegant supper in a private dining room at the tasteful Olympic Hotel. The highlight of Christmas season was going over to the Washburns next door with our children on Christmas Eve for light supper before attending midnight mass at Saint Mark's Cathedral. We hosted the family potluck dinner that included sticky rice, stuffed tofu, prime rib, salmon, seven-layer jello, pumpkin pie and Christmas cookies at our house with my sisters' families on Christmas Day.

The International District community taught me how to be an effective community activist and to have fun at the same time. The highlight of my work week was joining Bob Santos for Friday night drinks at the Quong Tuck Restaurant on King Street, now the site of the new Wing Luke Asian Museum. Other favorite watering holes where the I.D. folks hung out were the Linyen Cafe, Four Seas Restaurant and Bush Garden.

Bob was the District's beloved role model for many of the younger activists. It was a delight seeing him inspire students like Sue Taoka, who worked for many years as director of Inter*Im and then at SCIDPDA, and Elaine Ko, former director of the International District Housing Alliance and Inter*Im.

I lost my fear of public speaking when Inter*Im members Ben Woo, Shigeko Uno, Tomio Moriguchi and Barry Mar elected me the first female board president. The most fun part of doing community work was having the opportunity to get together with others to "recap" the community news at Bush Garden with Ben, Shigeko, Tomio, Bob Santos and Alan Kurimura. I considered both Bob and Alan invaluable community brothers.

Our most effective lobbying tool was the community reception, where we had an opportunity to form alliances with various International District stakeholders and educate elected officials and policy makers on the needs and concerns of people in the District. Thanks to Shigeko, we had the best food, even without having a budget for parties. She and others would ask community businesses like Mikado, Bush Garden, House of Hong, Tai Tung and Uwajimaya to donate food for these events. For many years, the annual holiday party was held at the Astor Hotel on South Washington Street in a space that housed the Nippon Kan Theatre, a thriving Japanese American performance hall before World War II. The holiday party, sponsored by the International District Economic Association, was

Jerry Lee, center, poses with Vera and Joey after the sale of Ing & Associates – Author's photo.

a favorite annual event of the Mayor and members of the Seattle City Council.

The Seattle Community College system allowed me to open up my world of learning. Seattle Central Community College Professor Rae Tufts motivated me to study urban planning instead of early childhood education. South Seattle Community College President Jerry Brockey's support of Joey made it possible for his architectural practice to thrive. We returned the favor by providing endowed scholarships, volunteering, and supporting Dr. Peter Ku, an immigrant from Taiwan, who became President of North Seattle Community College and later Chancellor of the Seattle Community College District. I was president of the North Seattle Community College Foundation at the same time Joey was president of the South Seattle Community College Foundation. Our 15 years of service there are memorialized in the nostalgic photos of the many receptions and dinners we attended through the years.

What goes around does come around. Joey was thinking of retiring before we were awarded the design contract for a new library at South Seattle Community College. We had already downsized and it would have meant gearing up staffing and paying for the firm's liability insurance once again. When Jerry Lee heard that we were thinking about selling Ing & Associates, he gave Joey a call.

Jerry remembered Joey spending the afternoon with him when he had just finished architecture school. Joey told me about Jerry after the interview and said he thought he showed a lot of promise and that it was a shame we couldn't justify hiring him. I told him if he thought that highly of him, he should hire him. So Joey called Jerry and offered him a job. Jerry thanked him and told him he had just been hired by Mulvanny Architects. Jerry remembered that kindness and gave us a very generous offer for our firm

50th birthday party, 1990. Front row, from left: Joan Yoshitomi, Dolores Sibonga, Vera, Sharon Tomiko Santos, John Santos. Back row, from left: Elaine Ko, Sutapa Basu, Ben Woo, Ruthann Kurose, Joey, Bob Santos — Author's photo.

20 years later. When we merged, the two firms had 40 employees. Under Jerry's leadership, the number of the employees grew to 500, and the firm established several other offices around the country and in Shanghai.

Jerry understood how food can boost staff loyalty and motivation. Every Friday morning, the entire firm would be treated to breakfast, and whenever staff had to work late, pizzas and other snacks would be brought in. Jerry's generous nature was reflected in the way he treated staff and by his numerous philanthropic contributions to the community. Jerry retired as CEO of MulvannyG2 Architects in 2005. The firm has been named by the *Puget Sound Business Journal* as one of the best architectural firms to work for.

The "community" that energizes and keeps me on my toes the most is the group of Asian Pacific women friends known as the "Women Warriors." For many years, these women have met monthly. The group includes Ruth Woo, Dolores Sibonga, Sutapa Basu, Mary Hsu, Ruthann Kurose, Sharon Tomiko Santos, Edna Shim, Velma Veloria, Christine Yorozu and Joan Yoshitomi.

Ruth, the state-wide political guru, is the one who started the group and handles

membership. Dolores, the first Asian American woman elected to the Seattle Council, is someone we look up to as "mom," always looking out for the interests of Asian Pacific American community, especially when she was on the Council. UW Women's Center Executive Director Sutapa Basu and former State Representative Velma Veloria have worked to stop human trafficking and improve the lives of Third World women. Mary Hsu, a member of the Chinese Political Action Group, helped us understand the People's Republic of China better when the "bamboo curtain" had just begun lifting in the 1970s. Ruthann Kurose was instrumental in helping move redress legislation for Japanese Americans through the U.S. Congress. State Representative

Cruising with Chinatown friends, 1999
– Author's photo.

Sharon Tomiko Santos is a national leader in human rights. Edna Shim brought important insight during the period of heightened tension between African Americans and Korean immigrant grocers in Seattle's Central Area. Christine Yorozu has been a longtime board member and advocate for the Seattle Keiro Nursing Home. Joan Yoshitomi, working for the Office of the Superintendent of Public Instruction, has been a long-time advocate of quality, equitable education.

We formed the Women Warriors group under the guise of being an investment club, but the true agenda was having a regular time to get together, talk about what we were doing, vent our true feelings and share a meal. I suggested Women Warriors as the name for the group because, to me, the women who were part of the group exemplify the finest examples of Asian Pacific women's leadership. There are many other women community leaders and pioneers, but what makes these women special is how they support, nurture and inspire one another in a non-competitive way. They epitomize the meaning of sisterhood.

We would meet at Ruth's house because her husband would usually cook us a delicious Chinese meal. If he was out, someone else would bring over take-out food from a restaurant in the International District or Christine would bring a homemade dessert. We would invite the men over for our holiday party at our house. Sharon and Bob Santos would put out a resplendent traditional Japanese spread for New Year's Day. We would go to Edna's home for our summer picnic and have a grand Korean feast. Often, it was just the KFC chicken Ruth picked up on the way home, but food was not the main reason we chose to gather. We got together so that we could recharge our energy and spirits, catch up on the latest information, and just enjoy each other's company.

For me, following in the footsteps of earlier community mothers and being involved with the Women Warriors and other community causes has enriched my life far beyond whatever material success I might have achieved in my life. Some of these rather modest individuals may not have recognized the impact they have made by sharing a meal or lending a sympathetic ear or uttering an encouraging word, but they are the ones I like to remember and honor as I reflect back on the experiences of a lifetime.

Thank you again to all those who have and will break bread with me. You are the reason for this book and have provided the inspiration for me to try and make a difference. You are the essential "*dim sum*" – bit of the heart – in my personal Asian American dream.

Chinese Holidays

January and February
Chinese Lunar New Year

April and May
106th Day After Winter Solstice
Ching Ming

May and June
Fifth Day of Fifth Lunar Month
Dragon Boat Festival

September and October
15th Day of 8th Month
Moon Festival

September 28
Confucius' Birthday

October 10
Double Ten: 1911 End of
Manchu Dynasty

Chinese Lunar New Year
January and February
First day of first Lunar month

It is the most important day of the year in Chinese astrology. People hang up new kitchen gods, light firecrackers and keep the lights on all night to chase away bad luck or spirits. The house is clean, all debts and quarrels are cleared. It is believed the first day of Chinese New Year will determine your fate for the rest of the year. To avoid having to work hard for the rest of the year, people don't clean, go out, and/or take the day or week off to visit family and friends. Visitors give red envelopes to unmarried children, and bring canned ham, dried duck or oranges to their hosts. My favorite New Year gifts from visiting Chinatown "uncles" were the silver dollars in red envelopes and tins of Almond Roca, many of which were re-gifted. As with other Asian holidays, Chinese New Year foods are symbolic homonyms with auspicious meanings.

Traditional Foods

• **New Year Oranges:** Eaten after the 7th day from Lunar New Year Day

• **Box of New Year Candied Sweet Meats and Fruits**
Melon Seeds: Wish for many children
Carrots: Cut to look like gold coins to bring wealth
Melon: Represents continuous line of descendants
Coconut: Warm relationships
Lotus: Endless friendships
Kumquats: Golden blessings/luck

- **Jai: Monk's Vegetarian Dish**
  Fat Choy (dried black hair-like fungi) Wealth
  Mook Ngee (dried fungi from oak trees) Longevity and immortality
  Gum Choy (dried golden lilies) Golden wealth
  Fa Saang (peanuts) Birth and Promotion
  How See (dried oysters) Good undertakings/tidings
  Long Rice/Vermicelli Longevity, money, beauty, culture
  Foo Jook (bean sticks) Many household blessings
  Tofu Wealth
  Mushrooms Spring
  Lily Flower Gold and Luck
  Snow Peas Luck and Money
  Gao (Chinese New Year Pudding) Aspirations
  Round shape Family unity
  Mochi flour Family cohesiveness
  Sugar Sweetness of Life
  Sesame Seeds Many Children
  Red Dates Timely promotions/crops/births

Ching Ming

April and May

106th day after winter solstice

Marks the beginning of spring. The house is filled with narcissus and yellow flowering branches. It is the happy day of honoring ancestors. Family gravesites are visited, cleaned, and offerings of food, especially a whole boiled chicken, and wine are presented, which is later shared by family members.

Dragon Boat Race

May and June

Fifth day of fifth lunar month

Commemorates the martyred scholar/poet Chu-Yuan who threw himself into the water to protest the corrupt emperor. Dumplings or *doong tai* are eaten to honor him. As mentioned in this chapter, this was one of my favorite foods.

Kay Leong Lew's recipe of *doong* from the Chinese Community Girls Drill Team Cookbook

5 lb sweet rice
3½ tbsp salt
½ lb Chinese sausages cut into 1" pieces
1 lb salted pork cut into 1¼" pieces
24 salted duck egg yolks, cut in ½
1 lb diced chestnuts, soaked overnight and cut in ½
1 lb mung beans, parboiled and shelled (optional)
½ lb raw peanuts, optional (but that is my favorite *doong* ingredient!)
½ lb dried shrimp, presoaked and cleaned
1 lb ti leaves, soaked overnight

1. Wash. Boil with 1 tbsp baking soda. Rinse thoroughly. Soak in clear water until ready to use. Rinse again before using 1 tsp of boric acid powder.
2. Wash rice and soak 30 minutes. Drain, add salt.
3. Place 2 ti leaves with sides overlapping, forming a triangle and fill with the following:

¼ cup salted raw rice, previously soaked
2 pieces duck egg
1 piece Chinese sausage
1 piece salted pork
2 pieces chestnuts
1 tbsp mung beans

4. Add several peanuts and dried shrimps.
5. Cover filling with another ¼ cup salted raw rice.
6. Place another ti leaf over rice, around and overlapping sides.
7. Fold ends and tuck under.
8. Tie securely with white kite string round and around and across ends.
9. Cook doongs in large pot of water, sufficient to cover and add 1 tsp boric acid powder.
10. Bring to boil and cook 6 hours.
11. Drain and cool. Makes 24.

Moon Festival

September and October
15th day of 8th month

The holiday symbolizes harvest and the love story of two lovers who were separated by their families and meet once a year. Romantics eat mooncakes and look at the moon in hopes of seeing the lovers. The Seattle Chinese community held annual Moon Festivals until the late 60s.

The Chinese Banquet

Chinese New Year is celebrated with nine-course banquets throughout the first lunar month. Other special occasions are also celebrated this way. Nine in Cantonese sounds like the word for "long" as in "long life" and is considered a very lucky number. For special banquets, only meat and seafood are served. The nine-course feasts of my youth are now a rarity because of the high costs/unavailability of certain ingredients and because of dietary concerns.

Bird's nest or shark fin soup
Roasted chicken stuffed with sticky rice
Peking duck or squab
Crab or lobster with butter cream sauce
Red fatty pork
Abalone and black dried mushrooms
Seafood basket with oysters, shrimp, fishcake with fish bladder
Sweet-and-sour pork or shrimp
Whole steamed rock cod

The banquets today include several vegetable and tofu dishes, which I prefer anyway. However, nine-course banquets are still the way to mark friendships, holidays, good fortune, marriages, births, long life and death. The round table and abundance of food make for a memorable meal.